Concept to Completion

Writing Well in the Social Sciences

Concept to Completion

Writing Well in the Social Sciences

BRONWYN T. WILLIAMS
University of New Hampshire

MARY BRYDON-MILLER
New England College

Harcourt Brace College Publishers

Fort Worth Philadelphia San Diego New York Orlando Austin San Antonio
Toronto London Montreal Sydney Tokyo

Publisher	Christopher P. Klein
Executive Editor	Earl McPeek
Acquisitions Editor	John Haley
Project Editor	Betsy Cummings
Production Manager	Lois West
Art Director	Candice Clifford
Digital Compositor	Elizabeth Wilson
Cover Image	©Toyohiro Yamada/FPG

ISBN: 0-15-503796-X

Library of Congress Catalog Card Number: 96-76123

Address for Editorial Correspondence: Harcourt Brace College Publishers, 301 Commerce Street, Suite 3700, Fort Worth, Texas 76102.

Address for Orders: Harcourt Brace & Company, 6277 Sea Harbor Drive, Orlando, Florida 32887-6777, 1-800-782-4479, or 1-800-433-0001 (in Florida).

Printed in the United States of America

6 7 8 9 0 1 2 3 4 5   066   0 9 8 7 6 5 4 3 2 1

for
Evelyn Brydon Miller

and
Louise Cougill Williams

Our Mothers and Mentors

Acknowledgments

We could fill another book if we took the time to thank all of the teachers, colleagues, students, friends, and family who have influenced our writing and the way we teach writing. The list would stretch from grade-school teachers to our current semester's students. We will try, in the interests of brevity and the conservation of paper, to limit our direct acknowledgments to those people who have been instrumental in the conception and creation of this specific book.

Because our mission is teaching and because our students over the years have been the motivation behind the ideas and exercises in this book—and then the subjects of the trial-and-error process that helped us test and refine those concepts—we first want to acknowledge those students who directly contributed work to this book. We thank Tim Carson, Krista Grella, Ruth Hmar, Jennifer Pepin, Michael McEvoy, Kevin Scalera, Alexia Trihias, and Geoff Webb for their contributions, first in class, then later for this book.

We also could not have completed this book without the direct inspiration, encouragement, and feedback of colleagues from both New England College and the University of New Hampshire. From NEC, Kathy Van Weelden provided invaluable assistance in helping us to understand and communicate the treasures held in a library. Chris Dale, Roger Hock, and Anne Agee also made vital contributions to the success of this project. A particular thanks goes to our friend John Halcomb, whose assistance as everything from intellectual sounding board to child-care provider has made this project possible.

For more than a decade, our thinking about how to approach research writing has been largely shaped by the work of Bruce Ballenger. Bruce insists that good research and good writing can and should coexist, and his thoughts on convincing students of this concept echo throughout this book. He also deserves credit for the central ideas behind some of the exercises such as The Idea Gallery and Reclaiming your Focus.

The halls of Hamilton Smith Hall at UNH have been a fruitful ground for the inspiration and discussion of how to teach writing. Of the many colleagues who have given us food for thought over the years, the following people have provided either specific ideas or more general support for this project: Brock Dethier, Cinthia Gannett, Dot Radius Kasik, Don Murray, Nora Nevin, Tom Newkirk, Donna Qualley, Pat Sullivan, Barbara Tindall, and Sue Wheeler.

We would also like to thank our editor at Harcourt Brace, John Haley, for his clear and efficient advice as well as Michael Cobb for his help. The following people were generous in their time and comments in reviewing the book: Andrea L. Richards of the University of California at Los Angeles, Steven Specht of Lebanon Valley College, Benjamin Wallace of Cleveland State University, and Bonnie Potts of Humboldt State University.

Finally, we want to thank our sons, Griffith and Rhys, who helped us maintain our sense of humor and perspective throughout this project.

Table of Contents

Chapter One

Why It Is Important
to Write Well

After assigning students their first paper of the semester we often ask all of the writers in the room to raise their hands. If we are lucky, maybe two people will tentatively raise their hands to just about shoulder level.

That's when we ask all of the others to raise their hands and we say:

"You will be writing this semester, writing a great deal, in fact, on this assignment alone. Writers are people who write. So that makes all of you writers."

They may believe that what we are saying is, in some way, true. Writers are people who write. What students often don't believe is that they can become good writers and that becoming good writers is one of the most worthwhile skills they can work to achieve.

Writing serves many functions, but, essentially, writing exists to transmit information—whether an image, fact, idea, or argument. Writing well helps make transferring that information easy and enjoyable for the reader. Bad writing gets in the way of that. The best writers in any field are the ones with something to say and a clear and engaging way of saying it. This is true of novelists, journalists, politicians, business people, scientists, and scholars of every stripe and discipline.

Ideas in isolation are only half alive. As a student and a scholar you have ideas worth communicating and considering. You want to be able to communicate those ideas as clearly and effectively as possible. The more focused and less cluttered your writing is, the more attention your readers will be able to pay to the quality of your ideas and the less frustration your readers will have trying to figure out your writing.

Undoubtedly you, as a reader, have encountered the frustrations caused by trying to decipher bad writing—and there is a lot of bad writing out there by both students and scholars. You try to slog your way through a

1

book or an article that is unfocused, wordy, filled with useless jargon, and poorly organized. You get the sense that the author has some interesting ideas to offer; yet it is almost not worth the trouble to try to haul them out of the poor writing in which they are mired.

Contrast that with reading a well-written piece that carries you cleanly from one idea and example to the next. If the writing is good, you may not even notice it because it is easy to focus your attention on the ideas, facts, and examples. When you do notice the writing it is for the grace and elegance of how the words are put together.

Good writing skills will serve you well, not only in this class and others, but also for the rest of your life. There are few professions that do not, at some point, require you to write. You will have to write letters, reports, proposals, applications, papers; and in all of these instances the processes and skills you learn from this book will help you keep your writing sharp, clear, and engaging.

Good writing is important for you even if others are not rising to the same standards. There may be times when you can get by with mediocre writing, though much of the time you will not be so lucky. Yet you will never be penalized for writing well. More important, good writing will allow your work and your ideas to stand out from the crowd of people who don't care to work on making their writing better.

The Myths Of Writing— And The Realities

We probably don't have to convince you further of the value of writing well. Like many of our students, however, you may not be convinced that you are capable of it. You should not allow yourself to be fooled into believing some of the widely accepted myths about writing.

Myth 1: Writing is magic. People who write well have an inborn talent for it, and people who do not can't be taught how to do it.

The truth is far different from the myth. Writing is not magic; writing is hard work. The myth of the writer sitting down at the typewriter, getting inspired, and banging out a masterpiece belongs in the same place as the kid coming out of the stands to hit the game-winning home run in the World Series or the dancer stepping out of the audience to play the lead in the Broadway show. It's great for the movies, but bears little relationship to real life.

Myth 2: Writing is best when it is spontaneous and it "flows." That is when writing feels the most like magic. Writing that is slow and feels like work inevitably fails.

Good writers work hard. Writing is a craft, a skill. Good writers do tremendous amounts of writing that they never use. They often write quickly and spontaneously, but only after having done a great deal of preparation and thinking. Even then, they inevitably return to the piece they wrote quickly to do thorough and painstaking rewriting and revising. That is when their writing succeeds.

Myth 3: Writing is to be feared. You can't do it, so why bother trying and risk being humiliated?

Think of a skill you possess, whether it is playing a sport, a musical instrument, or computer games, cooking, repairing an appliance, even simply driving a car. You may have felt intimidated at the prospect of even attempting to master this skill. And remember how well you did the first time you tried it? Think about how much your skills improved the more you worked, or played, at it. By now, compared to when you began, some parts of the skill must seem routine. You are able to spend more of your time and energy experimenting with new approaches or refining what you know. Yet, at each stage of learning the skill, if you had decided not to try again for fear of being humiliated you would never possess the skill now.

Writing works the same way. The only way to improve your writing is to write. The more you work at it, the better you will get. The better you get, the easier the initial tasks will seem and the more attention you can pay to the more sophisticated elements of writing. Think of how far you have progressed as a writer from grade school through high school. There is no reason to think that you can't continue to improve if you continue to work at it. Good writers never "learn" how to write. Instead they are always learning how to write well.

Myth 4: There is a formula for every kind of writing, and you could write well if someone would only teach the formula to you.

Although there are kinds of writing that require certain recognized formats, such as experimental reports, each writing task presents its own unique challenges and opportunities. You have to decide what you want to say and how you want to say it. No one can predict that for you and tell you the formula for achieving it. Instead, you need to learn a process through which you can approach any variety of writing tasks and complete them successfully.

Myth 5: Research means copying out of books what other people have said, organizing it in an outline, and then writing a paper from it.

Good research is not the copying of other people's ideas and information. Good research is a process of using the ideas of others to help you discover the answers to your own questions.

When faced with a question in our daily lives, we instinctively ask other people if they know the answer. Then, however, we usually decide whether the information others provide us is useful in answering our particular question. Good research works on the same principle. You use research to find out what others have theorized, discovered, or believed about a subject. But you then use that information as a foundation upon which you build the answer to your specific question. You use the information you find to make your own connections and to draw your own conclusions.

Myth 6: Revision is punishment. If you were a good writer you would have done it well the first time and would not have to work on it further.

Good writers value the revision process. They know that they never get it done perfectly the first time and that rewriting and revision are essential to improving their work. The problem is that as readers, we never see that preparation and rewriting. We see a polished, finished piece of writing instead of all the crumpled drafts surrounding the writer's chair. It is as if we would expect Martina Navratilova to win at Wimbledon without practicing until she felt her arm would fall off, or Mikhail Baryshnikov to step on stage for a flawless performance without hours of backstage rehearsal.

Myth 7: Revision means correcting grammar and typos.

Revision includes correcting grammar and typos, but it is much, much more than that. Revision, which often might more appropriately be call "rewriting," means considering all of your writing—from the central ideas to the individual words—and seeing if they work effectively to get your reader to understand the information you are communicating. Sometimes revision means altering the primary focus of your paper, or rearranging the organization, or rewriting paragraphs, or cutting or adding whole sections.

Myth 8: Every professor wants the same kind of writing.

Or

Every professor wants different kinds of writing and won't explain what she or he wants.

Certainly, writing for the wide variety of interests and tastes embodied in your many college professors is a challenge, and occasionally a frustration. It is also good practice. Throughout your life the audiences for which you write will change, and you will have to adapt your writing to meet the needs of each audience. This requires thinking about the needs of your audience, talking to that person about what she or he is looking for in an assignment, and thinking carefully about how your writing can best serve those needs.

WRITING WELL AND THINKING CLEARLY

There is another immeasurable benefit of working on your writing—writing helps you think. Writing is thinking. It is not simply the transcription of completed, polished thoughts. Putting your thoughts on the page allows you to step away from them, to examine and reflect upon them. As Jack Rosenthal, the editor of the *New York Times Magazine,* wrote, "Writing, whether clear or clouded, freezes thought and offers it up for inspection." (Rosenthal, 1993) That inspection then allows you the opportunity to re-think and refine those thoughts and ideas. It also allows you to see connections between thoughts and ideas that weren't obvious as you were writing. Writing will help you develop your ideas, and that development will help sharpen your ability to think critically and creatively.

Donald Murray, a writing teacher and Pulitzer Prize-winning writer, put it this way:

> "Writing is the most disciplined form of thinking; writing is the fundamental tool of the intellectual life. Write your life down and you can stand back and study it, learn from it. . . . Writing is a fascinating discipline of the mind." (Murray, 1991)

THE PROCESS OF WRITING WELL

Good writers develop a process through which they approach a task. There are as many variations on this process as there are writers. For successful writers, however, the process often includes some form of preparation, or prewriting, the research, an initial draft, and extensive rewriting and revision. Throughout the process the act of writing helps the writer develop her thoughts and ideas. As a writer develops and improves, she also often comes up with shortcuts for some parts of the process and refinements for others. The process may change slightly from one task to the next, depending on which step requires more work, and it may evolve a great deal over a number of years. Even so, there is inevitably a process that a good writer relies on to begin and complete any writing assignment or task.

The problem for students is that more experienced writers, such as professors, often assume that students have already developed and refined their writing processes. Or, the professors' writing processes may have become so idiosyncratic and second nature that they have difficulty explaining them to students. Also, in many social science courses, in contrast to writing courses, not as much time is available to spend on the development of a writing process for a particular assignment.

HOW THIS BOOK CAN HELP

The purpose of this book is to help students tackle writing assignments in the social sciences. Although much of the book uses as its model the writing of a research paper, the process we describe and the exercises we offer can be applied effectively to virtually any piece of writing.

Chapter 2 follows the cliche, "the best place to start is at the beginning." Before you start your research or your writing you have to have a sense of what your subject is and what more you want to know about it. Even when a professor gives you an assignment, there is generally room for you to decide more precisely what you want to explore and write about. The more clearly you refine your focus at the beginning of the assignment—including the realization of what you <u>don't</u> want to cover-the more effective and efficient your research and writing will be. This chapter offers you a number of relatively quick exercises you can use to help find a manageable focus for an assignment and a list of questions you want to answer.

After you have a set of questions you want to answer, you have to find the information to answer them. Chapter Three gives you a sense of the kinds of sources that are available to you in the library, including the uses and benefits of computer databases. It also explains ways to evaluate sources—to determine what information is the most effective and persuasive.

Even when you find a source that you think will be useful, the writing may be so technical or complex that you may be tempted to give up on it. Have faith in your abilities. You can work through any piece of writing and gain valuable information from it. The key word here is *work*. Sometimes reading takes work. But there are ways to make that work more productive and efficient. Chapter Four gives you some insights and advice about how to approach reading and how to take effective notes and paraphrase while avoiding plagiarism.

Finally, with your information in hand, comes the time to begin creating your own paper. Your best hope for success, however, is not to start on it the night before it is due. Chapter Five gives you some exercises to get you started writing, to show you how to complete a first draft, and, perhaps most important, to show you how to do thorough rewriting and revision of your work—from reworking the organization to doing a final polishing of grammar and spelling. We don't expect you to use every exercise every time you write a paper. We do, however, provide a variety of exercises with which you can experiment until you find the ones that work best for you.

Finally, there are three appendixes that provide information on specific potential sources you might use in your research, citation and reference formats, and special forms of writing for the social sciences.

The intent of this book is to help people writing in the social sciences. Your professor may be using this book with you in class as part of your course. You can also use it effectively on your own, as a resource and reference book when tackling other writing tasks, now and in the future.

Writing can be hard, slow, and frustrating work. Yet, it is the most effective way to develop complex ideas and to communicate them to other people. The more you do it, the more rewarding it will become.

As the authors of this book, we continue our lives as writers. We have used all of the exercises in this book either with our own writing or with our classes. The words in this book went through numerous drafts and revisions before the book went to print. It was not magic. It took time and hard work, but it was work worth doing. We both enjoy writing, and we enjoy helping people to become better writers. We know that all students have ideas worth hearing, and the most gratifying aspect of teaching is to help our students grasp those ideas and release them to the rest of the world. We hope you have good luck and good writing with this book.

Let's get started.

Chapter Two

Getting Started

There is a slightly perverse romantic notion among many college students about pulling an all-nighter to get a paper done and stumbling into class unshowered and wired on coffee to hand in the paper. All-nighters may be testaments to stamina and fear, but, let's be honest, you could probably do without the stress (not to mention that you are probably not doing your finest work at 5 a.m. on no sleep).

You know you will produce your best work if you give yourself enough time to do it thoughtfully and carefully. The problem may be procrastination. There is no doubt that it is deceptively easy to put off work on an assignment that won't be due for a month or two. Yet every day that you put it off the deadline gets closer, and you end up having to cram more and more work into less and less time.

Avoiding procrastination is not always easy. The fact that you are reading this chapter of this book now—assuming that "now" is soon after you received the assignment—is a step in the right direction. If you start working on your assignment with this chapter now and keep doing a little work every day you will end up with a much better paper and much less stress.

KNOWING YOUR ASSIGNMENT AND YOUR AUDIENCE

There is, however, little point to starting early if you don't know where to begin. Whether in class or in a job, you usually are given some kind of writing assignment. The nature of the assignment will set the boundaries for your work. Sometimes those boundaries may be very broad, sometimes very narrow. Regardless of what the assignment is, what you do after you receive it is crucial. A few simple, early steps will help you get on the right track and make your subsequent work easier.

First, you need to read the assignment. It sounds obvious, perhaps, but many students get started in the wrong direction by not reading carefully to make sure they understand what their professors are looking for.

Take a look at the following assignment:

> *"Traditionally, the field of psychology has been dominated by theory and research developed in the United States and Europe. As cross-cultural contacts become more a part of everyday life, we can see that our understandings of psychological phenomena do not apply universally. Review the research on basic dimensions of personality and evaluate this research in a broader cross-cultural context."*

First, find the key verbs. Find the words that are explicitly telling you <u>what</u> the instructor wants you to do. In this example, the key words are *review* and *evaluate*. What, specifically, do those words mean? And how are they different than *analyze* or *compare?*

Keep in mind these quick definitions of the more common verbs you will find in writing assignments:

Analyze: To take apart an idea or event or to experiment and examine the pieces to determine its nature.

Compare: To examine and discover similarities and differences.

Describe: To tell about in detail.

Define: To determine and state the exact nature of an idea or event or experiment.

Discuss: To consider and argue all sides of an issue or idea.

Evaluate: To judge the merits of an idea or argument.

Explain: To make clear the meaning or interpretation.

Illustrate: To make clear by examples or comparisons.

Review: To consider a body of knowledge.

When you see these words in an assignment, think about what the assignment is really asking you to do. The preceding example, in other words, is asking you to look at the body of psychological research in a specific area and to judge the merits of this research in terms of how the same events or phenomena might vary due to cultural differences.

If you find words in an assignment with which you are unfamiliar, turn to the dictionary immediately. You cannot give professors good information if you cannot determine what they are asking you in the first place.

You also should pay attention to other details in the assignment such as quotations or specific theories or articles that are mentioned. For example, look at the following assignment.

"In the Haney, Banks, and Zimbardo prison simulation, rights become redefined as privileges. Explain what this means. Give examples of this happening, both as cited in the article and in other research. Why do you think this tends to happen?"

In this example the professor is looking for a specific response to a specific study. In your writing you will have to include information and examples that you have learned from the research mentioned in the assignment.

If there is a quotation or specific example in the assignment, you should make sure to incorporate this into your paper. The professor put these details in the assignment for a reason, and you need to decide what that reason is and respond to it effectively.

Many assignments you receive will be rather broad and will allow you a great deal of choice in terms of selecting a specific subject on which to write. You are particularly likely to find such assignments for longer, research-oriented papers.

There are, however, assignments that will be much more specific in what you are asked to do. The second assignment is an example of this kind. You may not have as much choice in terms of your focus for the paper. Even so, you can still make good use of the prewriting exercises and advice in this chapter.

You may also have discovered by now that some professors have unwritten rules for how they want students to write papers. Others may make assumptions about how you have been taught to write that may be different from your experiences. It's not that there is a plot to confuse and frustrate students. It is simply that there are countless ways to approach any writing assignment. Problems arise when these assumptions differ from professor to professor—even if we don't necessarily recognize that these differences exist. Consequently, it is a good idea to find out if there are any of these unwritten rules or assumptions for any assignment before you start to work on it. We are not telling you to write only what you think the professor wants to hear. We are saying that a professor's preference for a particular approach or format is based on something he wants to achieve in the class and that you need to be aware of that before you begin an assignment.

EXERCISE

Questions About Your Assignment

Some of these questions might seem too detailed or trivial to ask about, and many of your professors may have no preference about how a paper is written or formatted. Other professors may be quite clear and detailed in their assignments. Still, if an assignment is not clear to you, why risk being graded down for something in the format of your paper that you could have easily avoided by asking a simple question?

- Who is your reader? What does your reader want?
  (This may seem obvious. Your reader is your professor, who wants a good paper. But, in fact, there may be more to these questions than simple answers.)

For example:

Is your reader an expert in this field?

Does your reader want you to assume that she has some knowledge of your subject? Does your reader want you to write from the point of view of an expert?

Or, does your reader want you to write a paper that an intelligent non-expert could understand?

Does your reader want you to demonstrate your background knowledge in the paper?

- Can personal experiences or reflections be included in your paper?
- Is there a specific approach or analysis (not defined in the assignment) that you should include in your paper?
- Are there specific theories, terms, or research (not defined in the assignment) that should appear in your paper?
- Will others—class members, perhaps—be reading your paper?

You may also want to make sure that you are aware of all requirements for the format of the paper, or how the paper should look. This may be explained in the course syllabus, or the professor may simply ask you to follow APA or MLA formats (these are explained in Appendix B). You should check to see if you can answer these questions about an assignment, however, and if you cannot you should ask your professor to clarify them for you.

For example:
- Is there a page minimum or maximum?
- What citation and bibliography format should you use?
- How should the paper look in terms of a title page and margin sizes?
- Can you use "I" or "you" in your writing?
- Can you use contractions in your writing?

After you have a clear sense from the instructor of what is expected in the assignment, you need to get started on it. Start on the day the assignment is given to you, if possible. The professor's instructions and your initial thoughts about the assignment will be fresh in your mind. Besides, getting started right away will put you more in control, rather than letting the assignment grow and intimidate you as you try to ignore it.

PREWRITING

The best way to begin any assignment is by prewriting. What is prewriting? Some people might call it "brainstorming" or "free-writing." Prewriting is simply thinking about what you want your focus to be. Different people do this in different ways, but almost all good writers go through a prewriting stage of some kind. It helps them sort through their ideas on a given subject. They find which ideas they want to keep—and begin to find some ways to organize those ideas—and they find which ideas aren't right for a given project.

Sometimes prewriting builds on your first thoughts and leads you in a different direction than you initially expected. Other times it confirms the strength of your original ideas and gives you a way to start putting them into words. This may sound at odds with what you have been told or have come to believe about writing. Some teachers and textbooks will tell you not to start writing until you are sure of what you want to say. Our approach—that you can't be sure of what you want to say until you do some writing—is the opposite of that for several reasons.

The first reason is that very few people have minds so well organized that they can construct a paper, word by word, in their heads and then transcribe it to paper. We all get distracted, our minds wander. If we get stuck in one sentence we may forget where the paper is heading; or we may be so intent on getting to the end of the paper, at the expense of good word-by-word writing, that the writing is skimpy and clumsy. We need to be able to put our thoughts, our minds, on the page, where we can consider them at our leisure without worrying about losing them when we have to start thinking about lunch.

Second, if you try to figure out exactly what you want to say and then carefully write out a specific outline, you lose the momentum of thought that creates new ideas. You get so involved in the outline that you don't open your mind to ideas you may not have considered. Sometimes we need to think fast, and the only way to catch those ideas is to write fast. Only if you shut off your internal censor that says that every word has to be perfect and useful will you be able to get a sense of the implications and connections between the initial ideas you have. Consider it like panning for gold. If you sat by a stream and tried to pick grains of gold out of the streambed one by one you probably wouldn't have much success, and it would take a long time. If, on the other hand, you scooped up a pan full of silt and quickly sifted through it you would probably end up with more of what you wanted in a hurry. In writing, you need to create that pan full of silt, then sift some of it away, to end up with the valuable things you want.

Finally, if you try to plan your paper in your head, make an outline, and write the paper in one draft you will have to be so careful with each sentence that you will lose any energy you have to give to the writing.

There is a time for precision, but it comes later in the process with revision. Also, if you are writing a one-draft paper so carefully, and the focus of the paper begins to shift, it is frustrating and possible grounds for a small panic attack. But, if your initial writing is fast and rough, you will find the diversions and digressions you encounter to be exciting and creative. When you are in a hurry to get somewhere, taking a wrong turn is maddening. If you are on a Sunday drive with no particular destination in mind, a wrong turn is an opportunity for adventure. Prewriting offers the same kind of opportunity to find the unexpected, but more scenic, route.

We believe in getting your first thoughts down on paper. It can be a messy process, and some of the results you get from prewriting won't be useful to you for any particular assignment. Most of the results will be very useful, however. The point is, after you get those initial ideas onto a page where you can look at them, you can winnow the less good from the good and then build on those thoughts that you find intriguing.

FINDING AND NARROWING YOUR FOCUS

Perhaps most important, prewriting helps you begin to find a focus. There is nothing more important to writing than finding and maintaining a clear and consistent focus. Focus is as important to a writer as it is to a photographer. If a photographer isn't sure what object she wants to focus her camera on, the most important object in the picture might be blurry and unrecognizable. If the photographer can't decide what to focus on, the people looking at the picture won't know what they are looking at. If a writer isn't sure about the focus she wants to give a piece of writing, the readers won't know what they are supposed to find out from the writing. You have to find a focus and then make sure you stick to that focus.

It is far, far easier to find a focus for your work in the early stages than to try to find information, write a draft, and then come up with a focus. It is really just common sense. If you find a focus early, you will have a much clearer sense of what questions you need to answer, what information you need to find. You will also have a sense of what you do *not* need to find and will be able to keep yourself from chasing sources and ideas that, although interesting perhaps, do not serve your focus.

You may become very tired of reading the word *focus* in this book, but there is no getting around it. Focus is vital, and the sooner you begin to find one, the better off you will be.

Of course, it may not be possible to find an absolutely clear focus at this stage of an assignment. You may have more than one idea that you like or a broad idea that you can't narrow further until you do some research. Even so, anything you can do to find a focus, to eliminate what you don't need to find out, will help.

How do you do it, then? How do you begin to find the focus you want for an assignment?

The first thing to do is to open your mind to the possibilities the assignment offers you. Every assignment is an opportunity to learn—even the ones that may initially sound boring. It is up to you to find the angle, the focus, within an assignment that will make it compelling to you. It is worth taking the time to find a focus you care about. Have no doubt that you will do better work on any assignment if you are learning from it things that interest you and that captivate your imagination and curiosity.

It means that you have to follow your passions and interests. It also means that you shouldn't try to outguess your professor in terms of what she would like best in a paper. The professors we know would rather read an intelligent, well-written paper on a subject the student clearly cares about than a perfunctory paper done by a student who thought it was the subject that the professor cared about but that the student certainly had no interest in himself. Yes, you have to stay within the requirements of the assignment. Don't lose sight of that. Still, you can find a meaningful focus within the boundaries of any assignment.

Real researchers follow their passions. They aren't trying to find a cure for schizophrenia, or to reduce adult illiteracy, or to fight child abuse, or to map the human mind because someone assigned the topics to them. They are worried, or outraged, or intrigued by a problem or subject, and they want to find out more about it.

Mary's dissertation research involved helping people with disabilities gain accessibility to important places in the community. Nobody assigned her this research. She was drawn to the issue because she was outraged about the insensitivity and injustice these people were forced to face every day.

Here is an exercise to get you thinking about where your research passions lie.

EXERCISE

Following Your Passions

This is a quick, but useful, exercise to get you started when you have no sense of what might interest you in an assignment.

Make a list of:
—10 things that worry you
—10 things that anger or outrage you
—10 things that intrigue you

(Note: These don't all have to be earth-shattering subjects. Be honest and list anything that comes to mind.)

Now read the assignment again, carefully. Would any of the 30 or so subjects on your list fit, somehow, within the assignment? You don't have to be sure how, but just see if the subjects on your list might fit an assignment. A broad subject such as AIDS, for example, has aspects that could be studied in psychology, sociology, political science, or economics.

After you find the subjects that would fit within the assignment, try to narrow them to the one or two that you would find the most interesting.

If this exercise does not work for you immediately, don't give up. Look somewhere else. Look through the newspapers or magazines at the library, browse through your textbook, talk to your friends and family. You are mining for ideas, and if you do this for very long at all, you will come across a subject that does excite your interest and fit the assignment. Remember, for most assignments you will be spending several weeks wrapped up in the subject you choose. For your sake, take the time to come up with a subject in which you want to be that closely involved.

EXERCISE

Community Brainstorming

One way to find a subject for yourself is to help other people find subjects, too. (This exercise can be done in class, but it could also be done on your own with several other students from the class.)

The premise is easy enough—fast thinking and fast writing. Get at least three people up at the blackboard ready to write. Then have everyone reread the assignment and begin to say out loud any ideas they might have for an assignment. Don't worry if you're not sure that an idea might work or be appropriate. Not all ideas will fit, but they all deserve to be considered. Speed is the key here. Don't bother raising hands, just get your ideas out as quickly as they come to you. If you see an idea appear on the board that sparks another idea in you, say that idea, too.

Everyone must participate. Offer any idea that comes to you, even if it seems obscure or if you don't know how it could work. Someone might be able to use it or to give you some other ideas about it. Don't worry that if you have an idea you like someone else will steal it. Two or more people can work on the same project and come up with vastly different papers.

After the board is filled with ideas, you can write down the ideas that might appeal to you and begin to choose among them. You can also look at some of the individual ideas on the board and discuss how those subjects might be approached for this assignment. As you talk about this, your professor and fellow students can offer advice about areas of the subject you might not have considered or about how to begin looking into the implications of this subject.

Now you have an idea for a broad subject that will fit this assignment. But if you set out for the library at this point you would be overwhelmed by information. It is better to spend some time thinking about the possibilities within your subject. Any given subject—AIDS, for example—has hundreds of aspects on which you can focus. It is like an enormous house, and you have to find one room in which to settle. In order to find that room in a house this big, however, you may need to begin by drawing a map.

EXERCISE

Mapping

After you have a subject in mind, you need to begin to narrow that subject. If you are going on a trip, an auto club will draw for you on a map the best route you can take. This exercise does somewhat the same thing.

Write your subject in the middle of a piece of paper. Without worrying about staying within the lines, start writing all the words that seem connected with that subject. It doesn't matter what the words are— ideas, emotions, facts, and so on—or that the words seem to be leading away from your subject. Just keep writing until you have filled the page with words.

Now, draw a circle around your subject word. Then draw circles around all the other words that you find the *most* interesting. Then draw lines between the circled words that seem to be at all connected—this may leave out some of the words you circled.

When you are finished connecting words you will find you have drawn a rough map of some of the more specific ideas you want to cover in your paper. You will also find you have eliminated other aspects of the subject that you did not find as interesting or that cannot be connected to the focus you are forming. When these ideas come up in your research you can recognize them and pass them by. You have begun to find a more specific focus for your subject.

If mapping does not work for you, or if you want to explore your ideas in more detail, there are other exercises you can try.

EXERCISE

Funnel Writing

Another way to both narrow your focus and begin to expand on and make connections between your ideas is called "funnel writing." Remember in the earlier exercise when you and your classmates put a "fast list" of ideas on the board?

In this exercise, you choose one of those ideas that appeals to you or an idea of your own. Then write for 10 minutes without stopping. Simply get your first thoughts about the subject down on the page. Don't worry if your thoughts wander or if the grammar isn't perfect. Just write.

After 10 minutes, read what you have written. Find the idea or ideas you think are the most interesting and summarize them in a sentence at the bottom of the paragraph. Using the summary sentence as your starting point, write for another 10 minutes. Again, don't worry about neatness or coherence—just follow your thoughts. At the end of 10 minutes, find your best thought and write a summary sentence. Repeat the process at least one more time, though two or three more times would be the most productive.

This exercise may lead you to a more focused idea that you can pursue for your paper. (The idea you settle on may not necessarily come at the end, by the way.) It also allows you to see other ideas and thoughts that may be connected to your focus. Read through all you have written. Underline or circle all of the ideas that are intriguing to you or that seem connected. Don't worry about everything else.

When you begin to have a clearer idea of what your specific focus will be, it is worth spending a little more time prewriting. These exercises will help you do some thinking within the subject you have chosen. You have an idea for your paper. But what do you know about that subject already? What are your first thoughts? Your biases? Do you know things about your subject that you don't initially realize you know? What do you want to find out?

Prewriting at this stage will help you to clarify the intellectual starting point from which you will begin your paper. It will clarify the questions you will need to answer and the problems you will need to solve in order to complete the assignment.

EXERCISE

Free-Writing and Focus

There are many names for this kind of exercise and many variations of it. (For a more extensive discussion of this kind of writing see Peter Elbow and Pat Belanoff's excellent book, *A Community of Writers*.) It can be used for generating ideas and narrowing your focus. We think it is even more valuable for exploring the possibilities and implications of your focus. What questions do you have about your research? What is your initial hypothesis? This exercise gives you the chance to get your thoughts down on the page so that you can step back from and consider them. It also allows you to form your initial thoughts and theories without the interference of other people's conclusions. Finally, it is most often writing you do for yourself. It is private. That way you can be honest with your thoughts, follow your hunches, and not lose the energy of your writing.

Some of the free-writing you do will be good. Some may even end up in some form in your final draft. Other free-writing you do will be bad, and, even if you keep the ideas, you'll pitch the rest. Either way, it gives you a point from which to begin.

Free-writing will work most effectively when you do three things:

1. Write quickly. Just think and let your pen follow your thoughts.

2. Write for at least 10 minutes at a stretch. You have to give yourself a chance to get warmed up and then develop your thoughts.

3. Don't judge yourself too harshly while you are writing. If you get stuck or feel you aren't writing well, don't stop! Go on to the next idea and keep writing. You will be surprised at the ideas that you won't like while you are writing that will look better when you go back to read them. Shut off your internal judgment machine and write.

The idea of focused free-writing is to take your initial idea and develop it. The easiest way to do this is to find a general starting point and then write. Here are some suggestions of where to begin:

Make a bold statement: Try testing the subject you have against the boldest statement you can think of. (And don't worry if the statement isn't true. Lies are often great for getting your brain and adrenaline working.) For example, if your focus is moral development write "Men have higher levels of moral development than women" or "The highest stages of moral development occur more frequently in technologically advanced societies" at the top of the page. Then start to write. Attack the statement, support it, be angry, sarcastic, defensive, noble; in short, write whatever comes to mind. Then write an opposing statement and do the same thing. You will clarify what you already know about the subject and what about it matters most to you, and you will get a sense of what you need to find out to support or attack the statement more effectively.

Write a letter to a friend explaining your idea: Start writing a letter. Begin with the first thoughts that come to mind when you think of your subject. They can be any thoughts-questions, examples, ideas, arguments. Simply write them down and, if one particularly intrigues you, try to explain it to your friend in more detail. Try to imagine what a friend would ask you about the subject in a return letter. This will allow you to see how your interest in the subject developed, what you know of it, and what you want to find out.

Write with someone else's pen (at least in your imagination): It is helpful to step outside of your role as a researcher and to think about other people involved in your subject. Imagine yourself as someone else touched by your subject. For example, if your subject is AIDS you could be a person diagnosed with AIDS or a physician or the surgeon general or a senator.

Write what that person thinks and feels about the subject. If you were that person would you be excited, disappointed, angry, bitter, happy? Why would you feel that way? What kind of information would you like to find out and would you like other people to find out? What information would you prefer people not to look into?

As you free-write, if you come up with ideas, questions, paragraphs, examples, or phrases that you like, circle or highlight them. Even better, write them on fresh paper. This will be the information you will take with you as you begin your research.

You have been primarily working alone on this project. Now it is time to begin refining and testing your ideas with the help of others.

HELPING OTHERS—AND YOURSELF

Writing is usually considered a solitary endeavor. We imagine the writer, lonely and secluded, working her magic. It is true that no one but you can arrange the words on the page. It is also true, however, that most writers work with other people before they finish the final draft of a work. Sometimes they brainstorm ideas with others. Sometimes they work on research together. Virtually all of them show their work to readers and get their opinions before it is finished. If it is going to be published, at least one editor will work on it as well.

Rather than fearing the opinions of others, good writers welcome them. Ideas grow most effectively in public and good writers know that good readers can give them advice and insights into the ideas and writing that the writers themselves might have missed. Sometimes a reader might be confused by a piece of writing you thought was clear. Then you know you have to work on that part. Other times, a piece you weren't sure was working well will be praised by a reader. That is most gratifying—and reassuring.

In writing this book, we talked and collaborated with others at every step of the process. Of course, we worked with each other. Yet we also talked about our ideas with friends and coworkers. By the time you read the words on this page, they will have been read and commented on by friends, colleagues, students, other writers, and the editors working at the publishing house. You need read only the acknowledgements at the beginning of the book to see how broad our influences were. Why would a writer want to wait until the final draft to show his ideas to other people?

Though there are more good reasons to work with others on your writing than to avoid collaborating, there is one very strong reason that some writers avoid talking about their ideas or showing their work to anyone but the professor requiring it:

Fear.

Writing is scary enough as it is. It is hard enough to take the ideas in your head and have to spread them out on a page for a professor to evaluate. Now we are asking you to show those ideas to the world before you have had a chance to polish them. It can be a little scary. If you are willing to take the chance, however, you will find there are many benefits. The more you let other people see and comment on your ideas, the stronger your ideas will become. You will be able to get a sense of what works and what needs improvement or needs to be eliminated altogether. Also, the more you see and comment on the ideas and writing of others, the better you will get at recognizing what is or is not good—in the writing of others as well as your own.

The keys to effective collaborative work are trust, patience, and tolerance. The principle behind working with others is that you are trying to help each other out, not tear each other down. You have to make your comments constructive, not destructive. You must also be sure that you are addressing the ideas and the writing involved and not getting sidetracked by issues of personality. Be sure to follow any criticism with a suggestion of how the work could be improved. Be equally sure to let people know what is working well and what you think they should keep or expand.

If it is your work that others are commenting on, try not to be defensive about their comments. Be sure you listen carefully to what people say and be sure you are clear about exactly what they mean. This certainly doesn't mean that you have to adopt all or any of the changes other people suggest. It does mean that you have to listen to them and consider them.

As you work with other classmates or friends and teachers outside of class, keep track of those people whom you find the most helpful to your work. When you find someone who makes clear and helpful comments and leaves you wanting to get back to work on your writing, hang on to that person and use him as much as possible when you write. In graduate school Bronwyn was lucky enough to be a student of the novelist Thomas Williams. Thomas Williams was thorough and often very critical of the work students handed in. Yet he was also very detailed in his suggestions and always left writers inspired and eager to get back to their drafts.

On the other hand, if you run up against someone who makes you hate what you are doing or hate writing, avoid that person at all costs. Another writing teacher of Bronwyn's would trash student papers to the point that many worthy early drafts ended up getting dumped by humiliated and frustrated students.

If a fellow student is not responding appropriately to a collaborative exercise and is abusing the necessary trust of others, don't let her get away with it. Talk it over with the student. If that doesn't work, bring it up to your teacher.

Finally, you may have had some unfortunate experiences with collaborative or group work in school. Perhaps one person let the group down by not doing his share of work. Perhaps another person tried to dominate what happened in the group. Perhaps there were personality conflicts. There is no denying that these kinds of problems occur in collaborative work. You should not assume that this is going to stop after you get out of the class-room. There are very few professions in which people don't end up working with others at some point; this certainly includes university scholars. Sooner or later you will have to learn how to deal effectively with people in groups. If a problem with the people in your group arises, don't let it go until it becomes a disaster. Deal with it openly and honestly as early as possible.

Often collaborative work on writing is delayed until you have written a first draft. We think that the sooner you get some responses and opinions to your ideas, the better off you will be. Take the prewriting exercises you have done and run those ideas and writings past your classmates and your teacher to see what they think of them. Are they clear? Do they make sense? What would someone else do with the idea at this point?

Here are a couple of other collaborative exercises that work a little differently and give you different kinds of reactions.

EXERCISE

The Idea Gallery

This works well when you can take large pieces of newsprint, tape them to the walls, and use markers—or even crayons—for writing. You can also do it with blackboards—if you have enough in the room—or, if you are using this book outside of class, you can simply pass pieces of paper around a group of fellow students.

After the newsprint is on the walls and the markers handed out, you have to write two things on the paper.

First, you write a one- or two-sentence summary of your focus.

Second, you list at least three questions you hope to find the answers to in your research.

After that, it is a matter of everyone standing up and wandering the room as if it were an art gallery—only this time people are perusing the ideas and questions that fellow students have written.

When you come across an idea that looks interesting to you, read the questions underneath it. Then, under those questions, add any of your own questions, comments, or suggestions about the subject and put your initials after your comments.

At the end of the exercise everyone should have many new comments and questions to copy and consider. It does not mean you have to follow up on every question other people suggested. It does expand the possibilities of the subject you are working on and gives you questions and comments to think about that you might not have considered. This exercise will give you a wide variety of short, immediate responses to your focus.

After you have considered the many responses to your focus that you have obtained through the idea gallery, you may want a more in-depth exchange of ideas about your subject. The next exercise will help you with that exchange.

EXERCISE

Take My Focus, Please

This exercise works best in pairs or very small groups. At the top of a piece of paper you should write, in a sentence or two, a description of your focus. You then trade papers with your partner, and you each take the other's paper home. Before the next class session or meeting with classmates you will read the other person's focus and then write at least one page describing what you would do if this were your focus for the assignment. Include questions you would try to answer, arguments you would make, opinions you have on the issue, examples you know of, sources you might try to find, and anything else you can think of. Take some time, think about it, and be as thorough and detailed as you can.

For example, if the legitimacy of eyewitness testimony is your partner's focus, you might mention an editorial you read on the subject of recovered memory, or you might recommend the student interview a professor you had for a course in learning and memory. If the student is doing an experiment on the subject, you might suggest that the same experimental subjects be asked to report events in different orders because this has been shown to improve the accuracy of recall (Fisher and Geiselman, 1988).

At the next class session you will trade back papers. Now you will have very detailed responses to your focus. Again, it doesn't mean you have to take all of your partner's advice. It does give you many different ideas and points of view to consider.

FREE YOUR MIND

We are almost at the end of this chapter, and you should, by now, have a clear enough focus to go on. You may feel a bit frustrated, as if you have done a great deal of work and writing, little of which may show up in your final draft. But think about how much clearer your idea of what you are going to write about is now, compared to when you received your assignment. You have been doing the vital work of revising your thoughts and clarifying your focus. Revision does not always wait until you have finished a draft.

You should be aware that you may continue to revise your thoughts, and your focus, as you do your research. If the information you find fits within your focus, that's great. If the information does not quite match what you had expected, however, you cannot try to bend it so it does. You are the one who has to be flexible. You have to be willing to adapt to new information.

It may mean that your focus will broaden as you do your research. That may be OK as long as you keep control of it. Think of it as having 50 marbles. It is much easier to count and control them if you have them in a bag and can take them out one at a time than if you start with them spread all over the floor.

You also have to be willing to have your mind changed. Good researchers set out on projects with flexible and skeptical minds. That means they examine each piece of information carefully and, if it tells them something they did not expect, they have to work with that information as it is, not ignore it or try to change it. Research requires a willingness to learn, to incorporate new ideas, and to admit when you are wrong. This doesn't mean you should not have unshakable convictions about certain issues. It does mean, however, that if you are so determined about an issue that you refuse to change your mind about it, it may not be the best subject for you to research. You won't always have to shift your focus as you do your research, but you have to be ready for that possibility.

EXERCISE

What You Need to Take to the Library

You should take two things with you to the library.

First, take two pieces of paper or note cards and write down on each one a sentence or two describing your focus. Keep one of the pieces with the notebook you take to the library and keep the other one where you write—next to your computer, typewriter, or desk.

Any time you are unsure if you are on the right track, check your note card or piece of paper. Also, if your focus shifts, tear up these note cards or pieces of paper and write down your new focus.

Second, write a list of at least 10 questions concerning what you want to find out.

You have your focus. You have your questions. Now it's time to find some answers.

Chapter Three

Finding What You Need

Seen any good movies lately?

If you have, think for a moment about how you decided on what movie to see. Did you see an ad on television? Or on a poster or in the newspaper? Did you read a review? Did you go on the recommendation of a friend or family member who had seen the movie? Did it star an actor you knew you would like? Did you simply go to the movie that was at the closest theater at the most convenient time?

However you chose to go about it, you were doing research. You had a question you wanted to answer (what movie should I go see?). You gathered information from outside sources (posters, ads, reviews, recommendations). You evaluated the quality of the information you received based on knowledge you possessed. (An ad for the movie said it was the best ever; but you wouldn't expect the ad to be critical, so you viewed its claim skeptically. Or, your mother said she hated the movie and you knew you would love any movie she hated. Or, you've always liked Mel Gibson movies in the past, so why should this time be different?) Finally, based on the information you'd gathered, you reached your own conclusion (*Lethal Weapon* it is).

Doing the research for a social science project is no different in its essential approach than choosing a movie, a restaurant, or a CD. You have a question, you find out what other people know that might help you answer that question, you evaluate the quality of their information, and you use that information to reach and support your answers to the question.

Research—good research—is not just the accumulation of piles of information, nor is it a slow death to be found in copying word-for-word from large, dusty books. Instead, good research is a process of discovery.

You use research to find out what other people know or believe about a subject. This helps you to gain the foundation of knowledge you need to draw your own conclusions or to conduct your own experiments. You get a sense of the range of opinions about a given subject. Consider, for

25

example, learning disabilities. What are the different explanations for the causes of learning disabilities? What are the best ways to deal with them? How do different people support their ideas? How did they do their research? Where have their solutions been tested? Research lets you identify the different theories and ideas about a subject and compare how people supported their theories with research. Finally, research keeps you from duplicating studies and ideas already developed by others; there's rarely a point to reinventing the wheel.

You use research to build on existing information and theories and to connect them to answer your questions. To answer a question about how advertising affects teenagers in their decisions to start smoking, you might have to find information about the psychology of advertising, about teens and smoking, and about teens and advertising, then draw ideas from all three areas to answer your question.

Most of all, you use research to provide you with the ideas and evidence you need to reach your own conclusions. The point of research is usually not the mere reporting of information from other sources. You're not doing book reports here. You are using sources to create new conclusions and knowledge. As you do your research, then, always be thinking about the information you are reading and how it compares and connects to what you have already learned.

Using, And Reusing, The Library

Like it or loathe it, you're going to have to go to a library. Frankly, it will be better for you and your work if you learn to like it; you'll stand a better chance of learning to like it if you learn to use it well.

A seventh-grade teacher once told me, "The library is your friend." It was the kind of comment that made me want to strangle her. Her analogy was accurate in one respect, however: As with any friend, the better you know the library, the more useful and predictable it will be; as with any friend, that level of knowledge takes time and effort.

There is, of course, a tremendous—if not sometimes overwhelming—amount of information available in your campus library. To keep from being overwhelmed you have to know how the library works, how to know which sources to use to solve a problem, how those sources work, how to use those sources to their best effect, and then how to recognize what information is useful to you in this project and what you should leave alone.

The library will rarely offer you a simple, one-shot answer to a research question. Nor is the library the research equivalent of Wal-Mart: No one-stop shopping here. You have to make a trip, obtain and digest information, think about what you need next, and go back through the process again. If you learn how to use the library, and use it frequently, it will give you the pieces you need to construct your own answer.

Think of yourself as a detective and the library as the city in which you are working. You begin with a mystery, a question you need to answer. The answer is somewhere in a city full of clues, dead ends, and solutions. You have to know where to look, follow your leads, persevere through the dead ends, go back and reinterview suspects, and be thorough in gathering your evidence to find your way to the truth.

You may very well be familiar with the general setup of your library and know how to use many of the more basic resources there, such as card catalogues and encyclopedias. We are going to focus on the resources available to you to do research in the social sciences. If you are unfamiliar with some of the terms we use or don't yet have a sense of how your library is set up, we strongly suggest you go over and ask how you can take a tour. Virtually every library we know has some kind of system of orientations and tours available for students. They are well worth the time and will save you hours later on. They can also put you in touch with library personnel who, as you will see in this chapter, can be exceptionally helpful.

There are many different kinds of information you can find about the social sciences. There are, however, a few important distinctions you need to keep in mind.

PRIMARY AND SECONDARY SOURCES

In general, information falls into two categories: primary sources and secondary sources. Both have their uses and some weaknesses. It is important to know what the difference is, though, so you know how the information you have in your hand may be useful.

Primary sources contain information coming directly from researchers, theorists, and so on. The information is the direct result of the author's ideas, observations, interviews, or experiences. No one else has diluted, condensed, or otherwise altered what the author or authors had to say. Using primary sources is the equivalent of making sure that you find out about a movie from someone who actually saw it, not from someone who just heard about it from a friend. Scholarly and professional journals, some books, government documents are all examples of primary sources.

You are probably already familiar with some secondary sources. Newspapers, magazines, television news shows and magazines, some books, and encyclopedias are all examples of secondary sources. A secondary source usually reports or comments on information contained in primary sources. In other words, instead of doing the original research, a secondary source will report on that research, often condensing or summarizing the information or comparing it to other research.

To say that primary sources are always better than secondary sources would be like saying drama is always better than comedy. Both have their uses; what is important is to know what those uses are and how to recognize which source is appropriate for what you need.

The clear value of primary sources is that you get the data or the theories directly from the authors without anyone else's interpretation. You know what the authors were thinking, what they were trying to prove, how they went about trying to prove it, and what they thought of their results. You, then, have the opportunity and the luxury of considering and analyzing their information without someone else's biases influencing your thinking. Think about how much more you trust a story a friend tells you about a party if you know that the friend was there, instead of knowing that the friend only heard the story from another friend who heard it from her brother who was there. You also can use data, examples, ideas, and quotations from the source to support your ideas. That will demonstrate to your reader that you have tried to gather your information as directly and accurately as possible. That will make your paper more credible.

Granted, primary sources can sometimes make for complicated and even confusing reading (though there are techniques we will discuss in the next chapter that will help you deal more effectively with such scholarly articles and books). Even so, if you want to find the most accurate and authoritative research, you will most often find yourself seeking primary sources. They are worth the effort.

Imagine that your topic involved investigating parent-child relationships; you would want to look for primary sources for firsthand research. In the February 1994 issue of the Journal of Marriage and Family, for example, you could read an article titled "Affection, Social Contact, and Geographic Distance Between Adult Children and Their Parents." The article, written by Leora Lawton, Merril Silverstein, and Vern Bengston of the University of Southern California, contains a literature review. (The authors discuss what other researchers in this area have concluded and how it led them to their project), the data from interviews with 1,500 adults about their relationships with their parents (including tables and charts to illustrate the information), the conclusions the authors reach using this data, and a thorough list of the references these authors used. By reading this article you would find out firsthand what the adult children had to say and what the authors believe this implies about parent-child relationships. You could then compare these findings to other research to draw your conclusions.

This doesn't mean that secondary sources are of no use, however. If you want to get a quick, broad overview of an issue, an encyclopedia might be a useful place to start. You will get only a broad summary without much in the way of detailed examples or data; but it could give you a wider perspective on an issue that you need. It might also provide you with what are generally considered to be important questions in that field.

A book or article that compares and analyzes several different studies could be an effective complement to reading the studies themselves. A popular magazine or newspaper might provide you with some everyday examples through which you could connect abstract theories to daily realities. Book reviews could give you a sense of whether a particular source was credible or flawed.

A book such as *Forty Studies That Changed Psychology: Explorations Into the History of Psychological Research,* by Roger R. Hock, is a good example of a worthwhile secondary source. He describes the methodology and results of particular studies in psychology. He then explains why those studies were important at the time and what their subsequent impact on the field has been.

BOOKS AND JOURNALS—DIFFERENT SOURCES, DIFFERENT USES

As you begin to search for sources, your first instinct may be to turn to books. And why not? Books are familiar; you know where to find a table of contents, an index, how the chapters are organized. Books are thick; you know that something with that many pages must have what you're looking for. Books are authoritative; any author who knows enough to write that much must know what he is talking about. So it is tempting to go into the library, head for the card catalogue or card catalogue computer, and emerge half an hour later with 10 pounds of books you are sure will answer your every question, but you are equally sure you dread trying to read them all.

There may be a better way.

Of course, books can be useful; there are more effective ways to use them than having to read them from start to finish. But before we get to that, let's take a minute to consider what books are best suited for and what you will find more easily in other sources—particularly in scholarly and professional journals.

The strength of a book is, obviously, the detail and depth of information it may contain. A book will probably cover an issue from several perspectives and have many examples. It will often give you a sense of the background or history of an issue. Even if this is not necessary for your focus, it may be a valuable perspective to have while reading and evaluating other information and writing your paper. Also, a well-documented book will have a bibliography through which you can begin to get a sense of other potential sources or even of some of the authorities in the field. That can help you search for those sources that fit more precisely with your focus.

For example, the book *Human Behavior in a Global Perspective: An Introduction to Cross-Cultural Psychology* has a bibliography—or "list of references," as it is usually called in the social sciences—that is 34 pages long. In this list you will find sources ranging from the journals *Memory and Cognition* to *The Journal of Cross-Cultural Psychology* to *Child Development* to *American Journal of Sociology*. You will find listed books from *Six Cultures: Studies of Child Rearing* to *Measuring Sex Stereotypes: A Thirty Nation Study* to *Modern Psychology and Cultural Adaptation*.

So what's the problem? There are several things to be careful of when using a book for research. First is the issue of timeliness. From the time an author comes up with the idea for a book, does the research, and writes the manuscript, at least a year to two or three years can pass. From the time the publisher gets the manuscript until the book comes out, another year goes by. Then your library has to see that the book has been published, purchase a copy, get it delivered, enter it in the catalogue, and get it up on the shelves—figure in at least a few more months if not more. By now, even in the newest book you can lay your hands on, the information is two to three years old. Be careful. As we will explain later in the chapter, when you are trying to evaluate the usefulness of a source, you need to consider how recent the information is. With books, this is a particular concern.

The other weakness of a book is the flip side of its strength. As we said before, a book will cover a wide range of information on an issue. Sometimes this is great. If, however, the focus of your research is much narrower you may be better served by trying to find specific studies more closely related to your topic.

Very often you will find such studies in primary sources such as scholarly and professional journals. For example, Krista's topic was the psychological treatment of male sex offenders. She found information connected to her focus in the following journals:

American Journal of Orthopsychiatry

Corrections Today

CQ Researcher

Journal of Abnormal Psychology

Journal of Consulting and Clinical Psychology

Journal of Counseling and Development

Journal of Homosexuality

Journal of Interpersonal Violence

Journal of Offender Rehabilitation

The information from these journals provided her with most of the primary information she needed for her research. The other advantage of journals is that, as with periodicals, they take considerably less time to publish than books. Consequently, the information may be much more up to date.

GETTING STARTED: FINDING THE RIGHT WORDS

The essential process of doing library research is fairly straightforward. First, you make sure that you find the right words to describe your focus. There are books to help you find the same words for your topic that are used to list articles about it in indexes and computer databases. Then you use those words and phrases to look up your topic in an index, database, card catalogue, or directory that will give you listings of articles and books connected to your focus. After evaluating whether that source is going to be credible and relevant to your research, it is simply a matter of finding the book or article and getting on with your reading and note-taking.

Whichever sources you are using, always be on the lookout for an intriguing idea, example, or, most important, the answer to a "why question." "Why" is the essential question in research. "Why has there been an increase in religious fundamentalism in recent years?" "Why does stress impair the ability to concentrate?" "Why are there cross-cultural differences in responses to basic perceptual stimuli, such as optical illusions?" Until you can answer all of the "why questions" posed by your topic, your work will not be complete. In the writing you have been doing so far to find a focus you have often been trying to answer "why": Why does this topic interest me? Why is this a problem now? Why aren't the solutions that have been tried working? Why did this problem occur? You need to keep that question—"why"—constantly in mind as you search for and read sources.

You also want to be careful to find a variety of sources and viewpoints. Do not rely too heavily on one source for all of your ideas and data. The more broadly you read, the more persuasive and well supported your paper will be.

Before you can decide which sources to use, you have to be able to find them, right? And to be able to find them, you have to know the magic words. These are the words that identify your topic in such a way that the indexes, databases, directories, and card catalogues will open up their secrets to you and tell you what sources exist related to your topic.

Yes, the cliche about this being the "information age" is true. There are mountains and mountains of information out there for you to use, and much of it has been catalogued and indexed to make it easier for you to find. If you don't know the right word to use when searching through these indexes and databases, however, you may never find the listings of the articles and books that may be just what you need. This is especially problematic if you are using a computer database. The advantage of a computer index is that you can narrow your search quickly by searching for several words in combination and you don't have to go flipping back and forth through pages of a thick index book. The problem is that computers are order takers; they can do only what you tell them to do. If you tell them to search for information but use the wrong word, they often cannot correct your mistake.

At this point, you have three choices: give up, try every word you can think of and hope you guess correctly, or look for something that will help you find the same words the people creating the index used. Luckily for you, the third option is the easiest and quickest way to get what you want. There are several reference books that exist solely to help you find the words that best describe your focus in terms that the computers and indexes will understand.

The best known of these is the *Library of Congress Subject Headings (LCSH),* which comes in a four-volume set. Most libraries have these books and use this system to classify and catalogue information. After you find the terms the *LCSH* uses to describe your topic, you have immediately made the rest of your research immeasurably easier.

Take your topic and look it up in the *LCSH.* For example, if you look up the word "Anxiety" in the *LCSH* you will find not only related terms you might use, such as "Fear" and "Worry," but you will also find broader terms, such as "Emotions" and "Neuroses," and narrower terms such as "Panic Disorders" and "Post-Traumatic Stress Disorder." (Figure 3.1 shows an example from the *LCSH.*)

Even if you are confident that you know the terms to use to begin searching for sources, the *LCSH* will give you alternative possibilities that could help you to narrow or broaden your search, or simply to find related material you had not considered.

There are other reference books, such as the *Thesaurus of Psychological Index Terms* or the *Thesaurus of Sociological Indexing Terms,* that offer essentially the same kind of help as the *LCSH* but that are more narrowly focused for a specific field. The *Thesaurus of Psychological Index Terms,* for example, uses the exact terms that are used in Psychological Abstracts (these are summaries of scholarly articles that we will discuss later in the chapter). Check with the librarian to see if any of these are available in your field.

If you plan to use a computer in your search, most databases use the same terms as the specialized thesaurus in that field or have their own guide to subject headings. The *PsycLIT®* database, for example, uses the same terms used in the *Thesaurus of Psychological Index Terms. PsycLIT®,* as with many other databases, also contains an index of terms within it that you can use at the computer.

Another way to get a broad sense of your topic, and to find words and terms with which you can search, is to look up your general topic in a specialized encyclopedia or directory. This is where a secondary source can be useful. By looking up your topic in the *Encyclopedia of Psychology* or the *Encyclopedic Dictionary of Psychology* you will get a broad and brief explanation of the issue. This information will rarely be sufficiently detailed or specific for all of your research needs, but it will help you to be aware of the implications of the issue beyond your focus and will undoubtedly give you additional words and terms with which you can search for sources.

FIGURE 3.1
Library of Congress Subject Heading entries

Defender of the marriage bond
    sa Promoters of justice (Canon law)
     x Defender of the bond
    xx Divorce (Canon law)
         Marriage—Annulment (Canon law)
         Marriage (Canon law)
         Matrimonial actions (Canon law)
         Promoters of justice (Canon law)
Defenders, Public
    See Public defenders
DeFenne family
    See Fenn family
Defense, Civil
    See Civil defense
Defense, Perceptual
    See Perceptual defense

As you do your research and continue to read, always be on the lookout for new terms or phrases you might be able to use to search for additional sources. Keep a list of the terms you have already used in your searches—this will keep you from needlessly duplicating searches—and a list of other words and phrases you might use. Also, remember to keep your focus card from the end of Chapter Two with you as you look for sources. It will help keep you on the trail of the information you need.

EXERCISE

Searching for the Right Words

Write down four words that you think describe your focus. Look up those words in the *Library of Congress Subject Headings* or the *Thesaurus of Psychological Index Terms* or a similar guide or thesaurus and write down at least five words or phrases that either narrow your focus or give you synonyms with which to search.

USING SOCIAL SCIENCES SOURCES

Now that you have a good initial sense of what words to use, where do you use them? When doing research in the social sciences there are numerous indexes, bibliographies, databases, and abstracts from which to choose. (We list some of the more common ones for specific disciplines in Appendix A.) First, though, we should take a look at how each of these systems works.

Indexes

In this age of computer databases and on-line services, the idea of searching in a book-style index for information may seem a bit quaint and certainly a waste of time. There are several good reasons to be familiar with how text indexes work, however. Your library may not have computer-searching capabilities—or even if it does, the computers may often be occupied by other students or not working—in which case knowing your way around a text index is a must.

The *Social Science Index:* Even when you can search on a database, a good text index, such as the *Social Science Index,* offers several other advantages. (The *Social Science Index* is available on a computer database now, but it still can be worthwhile to look into the bound copies.) First, the *Social Science Index* comes out frequently and has quite current listings. Also, computer databases tend to be narrowly focused—*PsycLIT®* includes only articles and books on psychology for example—whereas the *Social Science Index* covers psychology, sociology, economics, anthropology, law, medical science, environmental studies, and related fields and topics. By looking up your topic for a psychology research project in the *Social Science Index* you may find, in addition to psychology sources, articles about the topic in sociology or anthropology journals. These related fields may give you distinctive and valuable insights you might not have otherwise considered. Similarly, although searching in a database does allow you to do an efficient and narrowly focused search, checking out the text index lets you see the related article and subject headings that may spark some additional ideas. For example, if you look under "Learning" in the index you will first get a list of other terms you might use, such as "Conditioned Response" or "Episodic Memory" or "Reinforcement." Then you will get a list of articles touching on many different aspects of learning, such as "Conceptual Learning" or "Feedback Learning." (See Figure 3.2.)

Think of it like the difference between seeing a photograph of a single house, which allows you to study that structure in detail, or walking down the street it is on, which allows you to understand more fully the neighborhood in which the house sits. Sometimes it is useful to know who lives next door.

You may be familiar with using the *Reader's Guide to Periodical Literature*—volumes are organized by year, and the topics in each volume are organized alphabetically. The *Social Science Index,* and most other text indexes, work in essentially the same way. Other indexes are listed in Appendix A. If you are unsure about how they work or about the abbreviations, the books have instructions at the beginning.

The *Social Sciences Citation Index®:* There is another form of index that is vital to understand if you are to do research in the social sciences. The *Social Sciences Citation Index®* is actually composed of four separate indexes: *Permuterm® Subject, Source, Citation,* and *Corporate Author.* The *SSCI* contains information on about 2,000 scholarly journals and is valuable not only

FIGURE 3.2
Social Science Index entries

Learning, Psychology of
     See also
    Achievement motivation
    Conservation concepts
    Educational psychology
    Electric shock (Psychological experimentation)
    Semantic memory
    Transfer of training
Acquisition of procedural skills from examples. J. R.
    Anderson and 1. M. Fincham. bibl J *Psychological*
    rearn Mem Cognit v20 pl322-40 N '94
Constraints on learning in nonprivileged domains. R. S.
    Siegler and K. Crowley. bibl *Cognit Psychol* v27
    pl94-226 O '94

       Conceptual learning

    See also
    Schema (Psychology)
Comparison-based learning: effects of comparing
    instances during category learning. T. L. Spalding
    and B. H. Ross. bibl J *Exp Psychol Learn Mem Cognit*
    v20 pl251-63 N '94

for finding journal articles, but also for identifying authorities who have written about your topic. These books take some getting used to—and the print is maddeningly small. Still, they are absolutely worth the time and effort.

The best place to start is with the *Permuterm® Subject Index.* Like the *Library of Congress Subject Headings,* it will give you the words and phrases related to your subject. What sets it apart from the *LCSH,* however, is that it also gives you the names of authors who have written journal articles about that specific topic. So, for example, under the large topic heading "Depression," there is the heading "Children's" and the name of "Patton, W." (Sometimes you may notice that the name shows up several times on this general subject. This might be an indication of someone who could be considered an authority on this topic.) You can then turn to the *Source Index* to locate the specific article written by W. Patton and P.C. Burnett titled "The Children's Depression Scale: Assessment of Factor Structure with Data from a Normal Adolescent Population." (See Figure 3.3.)

The *Source Index* will give you all of the publication information—title, journal, date, and so on—that you need about the articles written by the authors you located in the *Permuterm® Subject Index.* It will list the other authors who have cited Patton's article in their work as well. This gives you both other possible sources to investigate and some sense of how interesting and influential this author's work was to other scholars. This does not mean, of course, that an author whose work has not been cited frequently by others has done flawed or unimportant work.

FIGURE 3.3
Social Sciences Citation Index®

DEPRESSION

DEPRESSION(CONT)			DEPRESSION(CONT)			DEPRESSION(CONT)		
DISABLING	---	▶LANGER KG	EFFECTS	---	LAUER RE	FAMILY	---	KESSLER RC
DISCIPLINA.	---	GOODLIFF.J		---	LOWTHER S		---	LEACH LR
DISCONTINU.	---	▶VANELLE JM		---	MECHANIC D		---	PINI S
DISCREPANC.	---	▶DOMKEN M		---	MOREAU JL		---	SEWELL DD
DISCREPANCY	---	OCARROLL RE		---	▶PARTONEN T@	FAMILY-EXP.	---	ASARNOW JR
DISCRIMINA.	---	MITTENBE.W		---	▶RABKIN JG	FAMILY-INT.	---	DEAL JE +
DISEASE	---	▶COPPEN A		---	SCHITTEC.M	FAR	---	FRANK E
	---	▶MARTIN RL+		---	SCOTT AIF	FARMWORKER	---	CIESIELS.S
	---	▶STRAUSS SL+		---	SHAPIRO DA	FATIGUE	---	FRIEDBER.F
	---	YANG YM		---	STEIGER A		---	KRUPP LB
DISEASE-AC	---	▶ZAUTRA AJ		---	SULLIVAN PF		---	LLOYD A
DISEASES	---	▶CUMMINGS JL		---	VINES SW		---	SCHMALIN.KB
	---	STENAGER EN	EFFICACY	---	AMSTERDA.JD		---	SCHWARTZ RB
EFFECTS	---BAZARGAN M			---	GREEN BH	H-3	---	INY LJ
	---	▶CREWS WD@		---	KELLY JA	HAD	---	WATTIS JP
	---	DAQUILA PS	FAILS	---	HENRIQUE.JB	HALLUCINAT.	---	GALASKO D
	---	DOCTOR JN	FAMILIAL	---	▶DYER JG	HAMILTON	----	MULSANT BH
	---	JIANG W		---	KENDLER KS		---	TREVES JA
	---	▶KLEIFIEL.EI	FAMILY	---	GILLEN RW		---	VIDA S
	---	KUGLER J		---	GIVEN CW	HANDBOOK	---	FAVA GA+

3291	3292	3293

1994 Annual Permuterm® Subject Index
Philadelphia, P.A.: Institute for Scientific Information, Inc.®

If you look up an author's name in the *Citation Index* of *SSCI* you will find a listing of how many times and in what publications that author has published during the period covered by this volume. Again, this can be a good indicator of someone with a detailed knowledge of this subject. It does not list the title of the work, only the date and the name of the journal. The *Citation Index* also will give you a list of which authors have cited the articles by this author. This is another way to find the names of other authors in this field.

The *Corporate Author Index* is set up like the *Citation Index,* but rather than citing individual people as authors, it lists associations, corporations, government agencies and other groups who write journal articles— the Veterans Administration, for example.

Coming into a subject cold makes it difficult to know where to look, whom to trust, and who else might be useful to your research. The *Social Sciences Citation Index*® can be a detailed and efficient way for you to get this information.

EXERCISE

The *Social Sciences Citation Index*®

Using one of the words you found in the *Library of Congress Subject Headings* or a similar thesaurus or guide, find your topic in the *Permuterm*® *Subject Index.* Find the names of at least three authors who have written articles about that or related topics.

Now, using the *Source Index* and *Citation Index,* find the names of the articles written by those authors and the names of at least three other authors who have cited those works. Then find the names of the articles written by those authors. You now have the authors' names and titles of at least six articles that are of potential use to you in your research.

Bibliographies

When we speak of "bibliographies" we don't mean the bibliographies you find at the end of an article or at the back of a book; though, as we will explain later, you certainly don't want to ignore those. There is another important kind of bibliography. In this kind of bibliography—which exists in its own book—an author has put together a list of books related to a specific subject. This may be as broad as the *Bibliographical Guide to Psychology,* or as narrow as the *Abortion and Family Planning Bibliography for 1991.* As with an index, the value of a good bibliography is that someone else has gone to the trouble of organizing possible sources for you in a way that is easy to use.

An annotated bibliography includes a short summary of each book listed. Some books may contain a bibliographic essay, which is similar to an annotated bibliography but is done in essay form.

One caution about using a bibliography: Because it is a book about books, make sure to see when a bibliography was published and when the books that interest you were published. Remember, you generally want the most up-to-date information you can find.

Computer Databases

In an age when you can do everything from banking to buying shoes with a computer, the fact that you can search for information that way should be no surprise. You may, in fact, already be familiar with using a computer to do research if your school or local library has a computerized card catalogue system or *InfoTrac* database. There are several databases available if you are doing social science research, including *PsycLIT*® and *Sociofile.* These are on CD-ROM. (That's short for "compact disc-read-only memory." In other words, the information is stored on a CD—just like music—and you can read it, but not write on it.)

There are several significant advantages to using a database. A CD can store enormous amounts of very recent information. The computers are relatively fast and can usually give you a printout of the information you call up, saving your pen and your writing hand a lot of work. Also, most databases, such as *PsycLIT*®, provide you with not only the title and author of an article, but with an abstract, or summary, of the article as well. (See Figure 3.4.) This allows you to get a clearer sense of what an article is really about. Databases also search and list articles across several years at once,

FIGURE 3.4
Abstract From PsycLIT® CD-ROM

QUICK REFERENCE GUIDE

To restart system	Press F7 (Restart)	A phrase A word root Internal or limited truncation (one or no characters)	Find: well being Find: famil* Find: behavio?r ; Find: norm?
To select a database	Use arrow keys to highlight database Press spacebar, then Enter		
List of commands	Press F10, then highlighted letter	To combine concepts:	
Database information	Press F10, then G for Guide	Use AND to narrow search	Find: symbolism and language
To use Thesaurus	Press F10, then T for Thesaurus	Use OR to broaden search	Find: wellness or health
To link chapters, books	Place cursor on <<SEE BOOK>> or <<SEE CHAPTER>> Press L (for Link)	Use NOT to narrow search	Find: advertising not television
To search authors	Press F10, then I for Index Type last name, then Enter	Use WITH to restrict search to same field	Find: crowd* with violence
To look for: A word	Find: hesitation	Use NEAR to narrow search to number of words in proximity	Find: computer near anxiety Find: expert near2 system?

FIELD NAME	SAMPLE JOURNAL RECORD	SEARCH EXAMPLES
Title	TI: Effects of rock and roll music on mathematical, verbal, and reading comprehension performance.	rock with music in ti
Author	AU: Tucker,-Alexander; Bushman,-Brad-J.	tucker-alexander in au
Author Affiliation	IN: Iowa State U, US	iowa state in in
Journal Name	JN: Perceptual-and-Motor-Skills; 1991 Jun Vol 72(3, Pt 1) 942	perceptual-and-motor-skills in jn
ISSN	IS: 00315125	00315125 in is
Language	LA: English	english in la
Publication Year	PY: 1991	1991 in py ; py=1989-1992
Abstract	AB: 151 undergraduates completed mathematics, verbal, and reading comprehension problems while listening to rock and roll music played at 80 db or in silence. The music decreased performance on math and verbal tests but not on reading comprehension. (PsycLIT Database Copyright 1992 American Psychological Assn, all rights reserved)	rock near1 roll in ab
Key Phrase	KP: rock & roll music; mathematics & verbal & reading comprehension performance; college students	mathematics with performance in kp
Descriptors	DE: ROCK-MUSIC; READING-COMPREHENSION; MATHEMATICAL-ABILITY; VERBAL-ABILITY; ADULTHOOD-	rock-music in de ; adulthood- in de
Classification Codes	CC: 2340; 23	2340 in cc ; 23 in cc
Population	PO: Human	human in po
Age Group	AG: Adult	adult in ag
Update	UD: 9201	9201 in ud
Accession Number	AN: 79-00362	79-00362 in an
Journal Code	JC: 1576	1576 in jc

FOR SEARCH HELP, CONTACT:

PsycINFO User Services
American Psychological Association
750 First Street, NE
Washington, DC 20002-4242

Telephone:
(800) 374-2722 (in North America)
(202) 336-5650
FAX: (202) 336-5633

Reprinted with permission of the American Psychological Association, publisher of PsycINFO Database and PsycLIT.® All rights reserved.

instead of your having to go from one annual volume to the next. Best of all, the databases allow you to cross-reference your search. For example, if you are researching categorization strategies for a paper on cognitive psychology, you could cross-reference by using the terms "Concept Formation" and "Prototype" at the same time. With a text index you would have to look up each word separately and then see what articles might match.

The computer will search for any word you enter. This means you can search using an author's name, the name of the institution with which the author is affiliated, or any other important word you can think of.

The disadvantage of using databases can be summed up in one phrase: Computers can't think for themselves. The computer will do only what you tell it to. If you spell a word incorrectly, it will search for the misspelled word. If you don't narrow your search, the computer will give you all of the articles concerning the term "Cognition"—that will run into the thousands. If you haven't used the *Library of Congress Subject Headings* or the *Thesaurus of Psychological Index Terms* or the *Thesaurus of Sociological Index Terms* or the guide to subject headings for that database, you may end up not getting any response to your search or getting articles on a completely different subject than you had planned.

For example, a student in the library wanted to do research about racism on college campuses. She sat at the computer with the *PsycLIT*® CD-ROM and typed in the word "discrimination." To her surprise and bewilderment she was confronted with article after article about experiments on how laboratory rats tell one item from another—how they "discriminate" between objects.

"All I'm getting are these articles about rats," she complained.

The solution was in the *Thesaurus of Psychological Index Terms* sitting on the shelf behind her. A quick check in that book revealed that she should be using terms such as "Prejudice" or "Racism" or "Racial and Ethnic Attitudes" or "Racial and Ethnic Relations."

Computers can't think. Make sure you do.

As we said, the great advantage of searching with a database is that you can combine terms to narrow or broaden your search. The important words to remember are "and" and "or." If you want to broaden a search, using "or" will let you do that. For example, you might want to search for articles that contain references to "Prejudice" or "Racism" or "Racial and Ethnic Relations." The computer will then search for abstracts that contain any one of these three terms.

If you want to narrow your search, which is often the case, use "and." For example, let's say you are researching attitudes toward women supervisors in the workplace. If you search for "Women" you will get 15,147 article titles.

If you search for "Employment" you will get 3,333 titles. If you search for "Authority" you will get 1,444 titles. But, if you search for "Women" and "Employment" and "Authority" you will get only listings for articles in which all three of the terms appear. In this case, that will result in only seven titles. Not only is that a manageable number, but also you that know the information you get in most of those seven articles will probably be information you can use.

In Appendix A there is a list of databases you may have in your library. If you are unsure, check with the reference librarian. Most databases come with relatively clear, on-screen instructions about how to use them, and libraries usually have manuals and subject-heading guides nearby. Again, if you run into trouble about how to use them, talk to the librarian.

The other way to use computers to search for information is through on-line services. Although such services can get you access to many databases at once, they tend to be very expensive to use. If you have CD-ROM databases available, they should meet your needs. If not, try the text indexes first, so, at the very least, you narrow your search and need less time on line. (On-line services work on phone lines, and, just like long-distance calls, the longer you are on them, the more expensive they are.) Talk to your librarian if you don't have the CD-ROM database you need and feel you need to use an on-line search.

Abstracts

If you have *PsycLIT®* or *Sociofile* or other databases available to you, you may not need to work with reference books such as *Psychological Abstracts* or *Sociological Abstracts* (usually called just *Psych* or *Soc Abstracts*). Even so, it is worthwhile knowing your way around them. You may not have the computer databases in your library, or they may be down or have a long waiting line. Also, as with the *Social Science Index,* using a text for your searches can allow you to see any more easily related subject headings and articles that could help you in your research.

In the social sciences, "abstract" is the term used for a summary of the focus, methodology, and results of research written up in a journal article. Clearly the advantage of using abstracts, whether on a computer database or in a text, is to see quickly whether an article covers material you might find useful. Abstracts also contain the names of the authors, the institution with which they are affiliated, the title of the work, when it was published, and the journal in which it was published.

Psych and *Soc Abstracts* work essentially the same way. As with most indexes they are organized by year. In the back of each volume there is a Brief Subject Index. There you will find subject headings followed by numbers that refer to an abstract of an article about that subject. (If you are unsure that you are using the most accurate term when you use the index, look up your topic in the *Thesaurus of Psychological Index Terms* or the *Thesaurus of Sociological Index Terms*. These will give you the same terms used in the index of the abstracts. If these are unavailable, use the LCSH. Also, the end of each abstract contains lists of "descriptors." These are words that could be used for further, related searches.) Using the number from the Brief Subject Index, which, by the way, refers to the abstract itself, not to the page the abstract is on, you can find a summary of an article about your subject and can quickly decide if you want to find the journal and the complete article. (Note: If the article interests you for your research, reading an abstract is not a substitute for finding the primary source. The abstract will not provide enough information for you to thoroughly understand and evaluate the source.)

There is also an Author Index to *Psych* and *Soc Abstracts* that helps you look up articles written by a particular author. If you have found one useful article you can use this index to search for others by the same author, or you can use this index in conjunction with the *Social Science Citation Index* to find abstracts by specific authors.

There are more specialized abstracts as well—such as *Child Development Abstracts and Bibliography, Animal Behavior Abstracts, Criminal Justice Abstracts, Psychopharmacology Abstracts, Women's Studies Abstracts*—that, depending on your focus, may offer you other places to look.

EXERCISE

Using Abstracts

First, using either a computer database or abstracts in book form, find the abstracts of the titles you located using the *Social Science Citation Index.*

Second, try to narrow your search on a computer database by using two or three words in combination—connected by the word "and." If you have more than three words you can use in your searches, try several different combinations.

If you don't have access to a database, use the Brief Subject Index in *Psych* or *Soc Abstracts* to find the listings of at least four more articles.

By now you should be compiling a significant list of sources and determining, through the use of abstracts, which ones may be helpful to you. See which journals your library has and get to work reading the original articles.

Card Catalogues, Card Catalogue Computers, and Books

No doubt you know how to use a card catalogue, and you may very well have used a computerized card catalogue system. (Librarians, by the way, call these systems "on-line public access catalogues" or "OPAC.") In general they are easy to use and help you search quickly for books by subject, title, or author's name.

Some computerized catalogues make the distinction between searching for a "subject" or a "keyword." (This same distinction is made on some computer databases for journal articles.) The distinction is simple, but important. A "keyword" search will search for words that actually appear in the citation or the abstract. A "subject" search will find books that are more narrowly defined by such a word.

Finding books in the library is relatively easy; you've been doing it since grade school, and the essential process hasn't changed much. You find the listings for the books you need in the card catalogue or computerized catalogue. Books on similar subjects in similar fields will be shelved together. What has changed is the length and complexity of the books.

Every semester we have students come to our offices after their first trip to the library and complain that they found 10 books about their topic and that there is no way they will be able to read them all before the paper is due.

We agree.

The point is, however, that the students probably don't need to read every book cover to cover to get the information they need. If they know how to go about it, and if they have the right books for their research, they can probably mine individual sections of the books for the information they need. Of course, some books may be so central to their topic that they will need to read them cover to cover, but that probably will not include all of the books they have gathered. The trick is identifying which book will be useful to you and finding the sections relevant to your research.

First, the cliche is right: You can't judge a book by its cover—or by its title. Before you grab a book and rush off to the circulation desk to check it out, take a moment to examine it.

Look at the table of contents. Do the chapter titles seem connected to your research topic? Do any of your key terms and phrases show up there?

Look at the publication date. How recent is this information? Does that matter in terms of your topic?

Turn to the index and try locating some of the words and phrases important to your focus. Do they appear there? Are there many pages devoted to the subject? Turn to some of the entries and see if those pages seem at all related to what you are doing (but don't worry about understanding all of the information on them yet).

Find the bibliography. Do any of the references look familiar? Have you seen any of the authors' names before? Any of the book or article titles? Even if you haven't seen the titles before, do they seem to be connected to your focus?

Read the introduction. This is where the authors will spell out the focus of the book and what they are going to try to prove or explain. They will also give you a sense of the structure of the book.

If, having done this, you think the book still looks like a good one to check out, you will now have a better sense of which parts will be the most useful to you. You can go directly to those sections, bypassing the information that is not connected to your particular focus.

Government Documents

Government documents?

What good would government documents be outside of a political science course?

Plenty.

Every year the federal government finances and conducts a tremendous amount of social science research, much of which finds its way into the government documents section of your library. Additionally, many other government documents, such as congressional hearings and census figures, may touch on aspects of your research topic. Government documents are detailed and authoritative and cover a vast variety of subjects. Unfortunately, far too few students take advantage of these resources.

The federal government is one of the largest publishers in the world. There is at least one designated government documents depository library—a place where the government sends documents—in every congressional district. Your college, local, state, or county library may have a government documents section. They vary in size given the size of the library. If your library doesn't have government documents, it still probably has some of the indexes of the documents. Then you may be able to get copies of what you need through interlibrary loan or by writing:

Superintendent of Documents
Government Printing Office
Washington, DC 20402

Most documents are free and can usually be obtained within a few weeks; though this means you may have to do some planning.

The great thing about government documents is that they cover such a wide range of subjects and information. That can also be frustrating. On top of that, they are categorized and shelved in a system completely different than anything else in the library. This is why they are usually shelved by themselves and have a separate library staff. This system is complicated and often confusing, and you will have your best success if you can work with a librarian to search for what you need. Still, it is useful to know the basics of how the system works and what indexes to use to search for material.

The best place to search for information about government documents on your subject is the *Monthly Catalog of United States Government Publications.* It is available both in text and on CD-ROM. You can use the Subject Index to search for listings that fall under your topic. (You can also use it to search for titles, authors, and keywords.) If you find any entries that look promising, write down the entry number and turn to the catalogue. The entries are numbered sequentially and give you more information on the subjects covered, the agency responsible for the documents, the date of publication, the number of pages, and so on. The publications are shelved according to SuDoc (for "superintendent of documents") numbers that begin with the letter of the agency.

If you are working with government documents or touching on elements of public policy, such as mental health policy or services to the homeless, you may want to look into the *PAIS* (or *Public Affairs Information Services*) index. It is available in text and on CD-ROM and covers books and periodicals about government, political science, sociology, and economics. It works essentially like the *Social Science Index*.

DSM-IV

The *Diagnostic and Statistical Manual-Fourth Edition* describes various types of psychopathology or mental illness and is used by psychiatrists, clinical psychologists, and others who must make determinations concerning psychological disorders. It describes the symptoms associated with all forms of psychopathology and provides a good first source if you are researching some specific psychological problem.

General Indexes

As we mentioned, you will have the best success in finding accurate, detailed, and authoritative information by using specialized indexes and bibliographies to find primary sources in scholarly and professional journals and books. For this reason, you will rarely have use for such general indexes as the *Reader's Guide to Periodical Literature,* unless you want to see how a subject is covered by the popular media. Otherwise, information in such general-interest magazines will not be detailed enough to be of use to you.

Newspaper indexes, such as *InfoTrac* and *Newsbank,* and indexes of individual newspapers, such as *The New York Times Index, The Washington Post Index,* and *The Christian Science Monitor Index,* may be useful if you want to see how an issue is being covered or what the latest day-to-day examples of an issue—such as the long-term effects of Fetal Alcohol Syndrome on cognitive ability—might be. These indexes are straightforward and simple to use, with any instructions you might need in the front of each volume.

Interlibrary Loan

Another resource that many libraries have is interlibrary loan. This means that your library may have an agreement with other college or local libraries to exchange books and copies of journal articles. There is usually a special librarian in charge of such requests. This means that you can greatly expand the range of resources available to you. Some interlibrary loan requests can be filled in days; others may take weeks. It is yet another argument for getting started early and planning ahead.

and *PsycLIT®* and you still can't seem to find the right term to describe your focus, then go to the reference librarians, tell them what your topic is and what you have tried to find so far. At that point, with a clear background of what you are looking for and a sense of what you have already tried, they will probably be able to help you quickly and effectively. They are talented people; don't abuse that talent.

EVALUATING A SOURCE

You have searched the databases and indexes, tracked down the journal articles and books, but before you can begin reading and taking notes, you need to consider one more question: How useful is this source to my research?

The first rule to remember when determining the value of a source is that you must approach every source with a good dose of healthy skepticism. Don't accept any opinion, fact, or statistic without giving it some careful thought and, if possible, checking the information against other sources. **Remember, just because a statistic or fact or idea is in print does not mean it is true, accurate, or useful to you in researching your subject!**

Here are some things to consider when you initially come across a source:

Publication: What are the purpose and audience of the publication containing the article?

For example, *The Journal of Personality and Social Psychology* is a well-respected scholarly publication containing many primary sources, whereas *Psychology Today* is targeted at a general audience with secondary, often watered-down information. Also, some publications have a particular political or theoretical point of view. For example, *The Nation* is on the political left, and *The National Review* is on the political right, while *The Atlantic Monthly* tends to be more centrist. See if the publication has a statement of purpose listed in the table of contents or with the editors' names. You can also check a reference book titled *Magazines for Libraries*. This provides brief descriptions of a wide range of periodicals, including their intended audiences and any possible ideological slant. Or ask your professor or the librarians about the purpose and audience of the publication.

Timeliness: When was this article or book published? When were the data collected? Often the more recent the data, the more relevant they will be to your research. For example, if you were researching attitudes toward smoking in public places, information that was only 10 years old would be of little use to you given recent educational and publicity campaigns and changes in federal and state laws. On the other hand, you have to consider the issue of timeliness in relation to your specific research subject. If your

STAYING ALERT AND GOING FOR HELP

Always write down all the bibliographic information of every potent
source, even before you begin to read it. Write down the title, author, pu
lication, place and date of publication, page numbers—everything—
every potential source, even if you are unsure that you will find and u
that publication. You never know when some new piece of informatio
will suddenly make that article important for you. Having already writt
down all the important information you need to find the source, you w
now be saved the time and frustration of having to go back to locate tl
source's title and where it was published. Also, if you get the bibliograph
information down first, you won't forget to do it later as you begin rea(
ing. You don't want to have to go back to the library later simply to loc
up the publication date of an article you once had sitting in your han(
(And don't get caught up against a deadline and, in a panic, make up th
publication information. That is plagiarism and will usually result in a fai
ing grade.)

Always be on the lookout for potential sources. When you find a boo
or a journal article that looks intriguing, make sure to look at the bibliogra
phy or list of references to see if there are other titles that might be of us
to you. If you are reading an article and the author often cites one specifi
article, make sure to note that title in particular. Always note where in th
library you found specific sources.

Several times in this chapter we have suggested turning to reference li
brarians for help. If you are having trouble conducting a search, or using a
database, or finding the best word or term to use in a search, or locating a
particular journal or government document, the reference librarians can be
invaluable. These people not only are trained to know how a library works
and where things are stored, but they also are information detectives.
When presented with a mystery of how to find a particular piece of information, they bring to the task resourcefulness, creativity, and determina-
tion. They are there to help you and are glad to help you solve your
research mysteries.

Try to keep in mind, however, that there are rarely enough reference
librarians in any library to meet the demand. Consequently, if you want
them to help you, you have to try to help yourself as much as possible.
They are well-trained professionals, and they are not there to do your basic
research for you. They are there to answer specific questions and to solve
specific problems.

This means that if you walk into the library for the first time and say
to the reference librarians, "I've got to do a research project on child
abuse. Where can I find stuff about that?" not only will they be unable to
help you, they also will be justifiably annoyed. If, however, you have tried
the *Library of Congress Subject Headings* and the *Social Science Index*

subject is social influence, a study such as Milgram's classic research on obedience continues to be important and should not be disregarded simply because of age.

Authors: Who wrote the article or book? Who collected the data or ran the experiments? Do you recognize the names of the author or authors? Have they published other works in the field? Of course, you should not ignore what appears to be interesting or useful work simply because it is the first publication by an author.

This is a good time to use the *Social Science Citation Index* to see if the authors have published other works or if they are cited by other authors. Or you can search a database using an author's name to see how many related articles that author has published. Have other students or your professors heard of the authors? Check other books or articles you have to see if the authors' names appear. Again, this is not foolproof; someone who has written a great deal could, in fact, be less credible on a particular issue than someone who has written only an article or two. As always, be skeptical, ask questions.

Accuracy: Is the work cited properly? Does it have a proper bibliography? Do the authors cite other sources or authors with whom you are familiar? Much of the research in the social sciences is based on data-gathering and analysis, and to try to determine the accuracy of this work without any background in statistics can seem hopeless. However, if you have taken or are taking a course in research methods you can begin to use what you are learning to weigh and consider the methodology used by the authors. In all circumstances our advice is to use your common sense. Review the entire article; do not be tempted to just skip to the discussion section and assume that the people writing the article know what they are doing.

As you read the description of how the study was done, ask yourself whether the methodology of the experiment was clear. Was the research conducted carefully, or do you see flaws in it (poor questions, unrepresentative samples, etc.)? Do the statistical methods and results make sense? Do the facts or statistics support the conclusions?

If the authors have used other research approaches, such as qualitative or participatory research, consider how they gathered the information from research participants. Who took part in the research? What involvement have the researchers had in the community that would legitimize their role in the research? How, and by whom, has the information that was generated been used?

Do the recommendations made by the authors seem consistent with the results they have reported? These are all questions you can pose without having to be an expert. If there are more complex statistical matters you feel you should understand, talk with your professor.

Remember that all research methods, including experiments, have advantages and disadvantages. All studies have biases. Your task is to evaluate the unique contribution each study makes to our ability to understand a particular phenomenon or issue.

Books: If your source is a book, check the table of contents, the index, and the introduction to see if it is relevant to your subject. Also check the date of publication and the authors' credentials. Finally, see if there are reviews of the book in journals or newspapers that might give some sense of how others viewed this work. You can find reviews of books by looking in *Book Review Index, Book Review Digest*, the *Index to Book Reviews in the Social Sciences,* or *The New York Times Index.* Don't forget that you need to consider who the reviewers are and what their potential biases might be.

EXERCISE

Evaluating Sources

Using the questions listed in the preceding section—about the publications, authors, timeliness, and reviews of your sources—write an initial evaluation of your sources. Find the ones that are the most recent, the most credible. Find book reviews of the books that look the most useful to you.

As soon as you get your hands on a book or article, start reading it. Read as you go. Do not wait to begin reading until you think you have gathered every last piece of information you need. There are several good reasons for this. First, the earlier you begin reading, the more you learn and the easier it is to identify and evaluate the information you need. Consequently you will be able to determine more quickly if a book or article will fill a gap in your research or will give you repetitive or irrelevant information, and you have the time to find the additional information you need. Remember that research is not always a straight line. You often have to double back to check on or to reread a source as your knowledge of the subject grows. Also, you will continue to come across new terms, phrases, book and article titles, and authors' names you can use for additional searches. Remember to keep a list of all of these. Finally, if you spread out the reading you have to do it obviously gives you more time to absorb and reflect on what you are reading. Research is not always a straight line, but it is always a journey worth taking.

As you begin your reading you may find that you are confronted with complicated writing and ideas. Don't give up. In Chapter Four we will talk about working through complex pieces of reading, taking effective and well-organized notes, and avoiding plagiarism.

First, however, we need to spend some time talking about valuable sources you won't find in the library.

SOURCES BEYOND THE LIBRARY

Although the library is usually a good place to begin your research—you will want to find out what others already have said about your topic—it certainly isn't the only information game in town. For some topics, there are more reasons to want to get out of the library than just because you feel as if you have been there long enough to start paying rent.

The ultimate primary source is information you gather yourself. You gather it, you evaluate it, you know the context in which you obtained it. It is immediate. It is also fun. Knowing that you are generating knowledge is invigorating and exciting. It is what research is all about.

You may be using this text as part of a course in research methods. If so, you will be learning a great deal about conducting experiments, and this book is not intended as a substitute for a text on statistics and research methods—our focus is on writing. There are, however, other equally valid ways of generating knowledge that are generally given short shrift in such texts. We cannot provide a thorough introduction to the wide array of qualitative and participatory methods available. Yet, given that they do not receive much consideration in many texts on research methods, we believe it is important to mention the most important ideas involved in interviews, informal surveys, observations, and participatory research. Also, these are methods of gathering information that may be particularly valuable in social science courses outside of research methods.

Interviews

When Geoff was doing his paper on the effectiveness of government-financed rehabilitation centers, he knew that his work would be more accurate and credible if he interviewed the director of such a center. That way he could find out if some of the problems brought up in his written sources were the same ones happening to a rehabilitation center near his community. Not only did the information he gained in his interview confirm some of the conclusions he had been reaching through his reading, but the director also provided him with several detailed, firsthand examples that strengthened Geoff's paper.

In a sense, we are all conducting informal interviews all the time. We talk to people, ask them questions about ideas that interest us, and listen to their answers. An interview is nothing more than a structured, focused conversation. It is that simple. There are, however, several pieces of advice you can follow to make an interview more effective.

You are almost always better off waiting to do an interview until you have done a good chunk of library searching and reading. In the first place, that will give you the background you need to ask good, detailed questions and get good, detailed answers. When Bronwyn was a journalist, his first move after being assigned a story was to go to the newspaper's library and get all the background he could on the subject. Good background will keep you from asking obvious or irrelevant questions. You don't want to waste your time or the time of the person you are interviewing.

In the second place, after you have done some reading you will have a better sense of the people you want to interview. Knowing what holes you need to fill will help you find the most useful interview sources.

For example, you may want to interview an expert on the subject to get the most up-to-date information possible. Or you may want to interview an expert to get additional or opposing views and opinions about your focus. Or an expert might be able to answer questions that your reading has raised or that you don't understand. Or you may want to find examples to illustrate or support ideas you've gained from your reading; a wide range of people, expert and nonexpert, may be able to serve as sources for this kind of interview.

After you have decided on the purpose of your interview, you need to think about the right person to be your source. Not everyone connected with a subject will be the right person for your needs. Your best friend may have strongly held views about divorce, but he couldn't be considered an expert on whether children whose parents are in the midst of a divorce suffer more developmental problems in school. On the other hand, if your best friend's parents were divorced while he was in grade school and his grades suffered enough that year that he had to repeat third grade, he may still not be an expert in the field, but he may provide an excellent anecdotal example for your research. So, once again, you may need to do a little research to save yourself and your sources time.

If you are seeking experts on your subject, the first thing to do is to keep your eyes open while you are reading. If you keep coming across the name of one author who seems to be particularly well informed about your focus, check to see where that author is located, with what institution she is affiliated. You may be surprised to find her on your campus or at a nearby college or research institution. Even if she is far away, if she is perfectly suited to your needs she may be worth a phone call or letter.

Keep in mind that any college campus is also a research institution. If you are looking for someone on campus, check the faculty directory. Many colleges put out a directory that lists faculty members by their research and teaching interests. You look up your subject and find the people on your campus who specialize in that area. If your school does not have a faculty directory, look in the latest course schedule to see who is teaching what courses. A professor teaching a course titled Race and Ethnic Relations probably will have a few things to say on the subject of racism. If that still offers you no luck, go to the secretary or administrative assistant of the department most likely to cover your topic. He will probably have a list of the courses and research interests of the professors in the department (and he should also have a list of their office hours).

You may need to find experts off campus. One obvious place to look is the phone book. Therapists, counselors, and psychiatrists are listed in the Yellow Pages, for example, and many of them indicate their specialties, such as marriage counseling, child and adolescent counseling, phobias, depression, or eating disorders.

Another source of experts is the *Encyclopedia of Associations*. If there is a subject in this country, there is a group or association connected with it—from incest survivors to groups on both sides of issues such as capital punishment. The *Encyclopedia of Associations* lists the name of a group and gives a short description of that group's purpose, its publications, and its membership and lists the address and phone number. You may find a group connected to your subject in your area. If not, a call to the organization may connect you with local members or with experts you can interview by phone or mail, or the group might have information about your subject it can send you.

Finally, the best way to track down a source often is to ask. Ask your professor for ideas about people to interview. Ask your friends and roommates. Your best friend's mother may be a legislator on a committee dealing with mental health issues, and that may be just the source you need.

EXERCISE

Finding an Interview Subject

Make a list of the kinds of information—examples, opinions, data, and so on—you would like to obtain through an interview. Be as specific as possible. Now try to come up with the kinds of people who might be able to provide that information. Using your college's faculty directory, your written sources, the phone book, or the *Encyclopedia of Associations* or by asking around, come up with the names and phone numbers of at least three people who could be potential interview sources.

After you have found the person you want to interview, you need to arrange the interview. It is only natural to feel a bit nervous about asking someone for an interview. Try to remember this: Most people like to talk about issues that interest them. You won't have much trouble getting people to voice their opinions on topics, particularly if you give them a sense that you have already done some research.

When you call a source for an interview, be precise and clear about who you are and what you want. Introduce yourself, explain the purpose of the interview, and give a brief sense of what kind of information you would like the source to provide.

For example: "Hello, Professor Bridgewater. My name is _____, and I am writing a research paper about childhood memories for my child development class. I was wondering if I might be able to interview you about the concept of reconstructive memory?"

If the person agrees to the interview, set up a time—try to set up at least a half-hour appointment, get directions to the person's office, and say, "thank you." If the person says that he is not the best source to interview on this subject or is too busy, ask if he could recommend someone else you might contact for an interview.

After your appointment is arranged, you must then begin constructing effective questions. Computer programmers have a saying about their work: "Garbage in, garbage out." In other words, the information you get will be only as good as the information you put in. Interviews work the same way. The better your questions are, the better the answers you get will be. A well-prepared interviewer will gain the respect of the person being interviewed and will gather useful and interesting information.

In general, you want interview questions to be open-ended and fair. Open-ended questions are ones that can't be answered with a simple "yes" or "no." So, instead of asking, "Have out-patient mental health programs been successful in your community?" ask, "How would you evaluate the out-patient mental health programs in your community?" The first question may get you only a one-word answer; the second will get you a more thoughtful, detailed response.

Journalists are taught to look for the "five w's and the h"-who, what, where, when, why, and how. You, on the other hand, will probably be most interested in questions beginning with the last two words: how and why. In your research, as in virtually all academic research, you are looking for reasons; you are trying to figure out how things work or how people think or why events happen or why people act as they do. Of course, you don't have to restrict yourself to how and why, but the success you have in finding the reasons behind your topic will be greater if a substantial number of your questions use these words.

Finally, you want to avoid loaded questions: "Don't you think recent government programs for the homeless are a disaster?" or "Why is Prozac so overprescribed for clients with depression?" Remember that you are trying to find out what this person knows, not trying to impress her with your knowledge or opinions. Sometimes, if you disagree, it may be difficult to keep still while listening to someone else's views. Still, during the interview you have to be fair and not resort to cheap tricks. You can always refute someone's views in your paper.

Try to come up with at least 10 good, open-ended questions before you go to your interview. Write them down. Rewrite them, if necessary, so that they are clear and easy to understand when you read them aloud. Organize them so that related questions are next to each other. If you write down your questions and organize them well, you will save yourself the trouble of having to keep them straight in your head during your interview. Instead, you can keep your attention focused on what your source is saying, confident that your next question is in your notebook. The less you stumble around trying to think of what to ask next, the more in control of the interview you will remain.

EXERCISE

Building Interview Questions

Write down at least 15 questions you would like to ask the subject of your interview. Now choose the best of those questions and rewrite them so that they are clear and easy to read out loud. Finally, organize the questions by subject.

Don't confuse the interview you will be doing with what you see Mike Wallace and Sam Donaldson doing on television. You are not trying to uncover government corruption or bank fraud. You are trying to have a pleasant, informative, intelligent conversation. Although most people are happy to discuss their areas of expertise, they also are often intimidated by the idea of being questioned and quoted. You want to put them at ease, not nail them to the wall.

On the day of your interview make sure you get to your appointment on time—nobody likes to be kept waiting. Reintroduce yourself and restate the purpose and focus of the interview.

(Note: Unless you are an exceptionally fast and accurate note-taker, you should try to tape the interview. Before going to the appointment, check to see if your machine and tapes are working and have fresh batteries. After introducing yourself, ask if you may tape the interview for greater accuracy. Even as you are taping the interview, try to take accurate notes. Never fully trust any machine. Also, your notes will help you more easily locate specific sections of tape later on. When the interview is over, check your tape immediately to see if it was working. If not, do your best to go over your notes, make sure they make sense, and fill in any missing words while they are fresh in your mind.)

Ask any necessary background or biographical questions first. Then go on to your list of open-ended "how" and "why" questions. Follow your questions in order, but be ready to ask a follow-up question if your source says something you want to know more about. Also, make sure you understand everything your source is saying. It is far better to be honest about your confusion during the interview—for example, "I'm not sure about the meaning of the word you just used, `stratification.' Could you explain that for me?"—than to be in the middle of writing your paper and to realize you have no idea what the person was talking about.

When you have asked all of your questions and are sure you understand the answers, there is always one more question you should ask: "Is there anything else you think I should know about this subject?" You will be surprised at the amazing information that can come out of that simple question—information that your source hasn't told you because you didn't ask about it directly. She may assume you already had the information. If she says, "No, I think we've covered it all," then you can leave the interview with a sense of confidence. Finally, ask if you can contact the person again if you need any clarifications as you review your notes. Then say, "Thank you."

As soon as possible after the interview, review your notes, listen to your tape, get a sense of what information you have. Note the quotes that are the most intriguing or informative and transcribe them from your tape to paper if you can. The sooner you do it, the fresher it will be in your mind. It will also tip you off if you need any immediate clarifications.

Informal Surveys

Although it is unlikely that you will be doing any formal data-gathering and analysis for your paper, you may want to include the results of some informal research as a way of giving your work more weight and providing a better sense of the situation in your own area. As an example, Mary has had students study the attitudes of first-year students toward living in a residence hall exclusively with other first-year students. No other source of information will tell us as much as a survey of these students' attitudes.

Although you may not be able to draw a random sample or to create a professional survey, the experience of generating and analyzing information is still valuable; and the information generated through such an exercise can still be informative and useful.

As we noted in the discussion of interviewing, the key to a good survey is to ask the right people the right questions. Try to get a representative sample of the people whose attitudes you want to describe. Surveying ten of your closest friends will probably not provide as good a representative sample as will surveying a student from every other room in the building. Ask questions that allow the respondents to tell you how they are thinking and feeling. As noted earlier, avoid loaded questions and be sure you offer choices of possible responses that reflect an entire range of opinion. For example, consider:

> *"Do you think first-year dorms were a bad idea? Answer 'definitely yes' or 'most of the time.'"*

This question is poorly worded question and doesn't offer enough choices for response.

A better question would be:

> *"How would you describe your feelings toward living in a first-year dorm? Very satisfied, somewhat satisfied, somewhat dissatisfied, very dissatisfied, no opinion."*

If you want to conduct a more scientific and statistically valid survey, you will need to talk with your professor or refer to a book that discusses research methods in more depth than we can here.

Observational Research

You may also consider doing some observational research. Again, let's say that you are interested in studying the issue of first-year residence halls. Perhaps you could spend time checking to see who uses the dorm lounges and for what purposes. You want to be as unobtrusive as possible. For example, don't go sit in the lounge and see who comes in, because this might influence who does. Instead, walk by at regular intervals and note carefully who is there and what they are doing. Make observations over a number of different days and times. If you want to compare observations of two different settings, be sure that you do it in a way that allows for fair comparisons. Comparing first-year dorm lounges on a Monday morning to integrated lounges on a Thursday afternoon is probably going to be misleading. When you write, be sure to explain, in detail, how you conducted your observations.

Other methods, such as looking at records that have been kept or looking at traces that people leave behind, can also be informative.

Participatory Research

Another approach to research that you might consider is participatory research. It involves working with members of a community to address the issues that concern them. The researcher provides technical expertise; the community members provide their knowledge of the problem and its effects on their lives and on the lives of those close to them. One researcher helped members of a Latino community in Manchester, New Hampshire, to survey its members in order to identify the problems that they thought were the most pressing to their community. They then used the results of the survey to lobby local authorities for Spanish-language AIDS education (Dale, 1993).

In general, participatory research takes a great deal of time and a long-term commitment to the community with which you are working. These costs, however, are outweighed by the benefits, both in your understanding of the issue and in the tangible contribution you can make toward addressing important issues.

As we mentioned, if you want to pursue these or any other methods you should look into a research methods book or alternative research methods book. We list several such books in Appendix A.

THE RIGHT TIME TO WRITE

By now you should have an ocean of information in front of you. Yet, it is no good to you until you can read and evaluate it carefully, take effective notes, and organize those ideas. It is time to take the plunge.

Chapter Four

Creative Reading

Imagine for a moment that you are strolling across campus and come across a bookbag sitting on a bench. You're an honest and helpful person and, in an attempt to find the owner of the bag, you open it and examine the contents. You find an economics textbook, two notebooks, a half-empty package of breath mints, a library book about Shakespeare, a hairbrush, a pair of sunglasses, a set of keys—including a dorm room key, mailbox key, and a Toyota key—on a keychain shaped like Mickey Mouse, a wallet with an out-of-state driver's license, an ATM card, the phone number of a dentist, photos of two young women and one young man, three dollars, a student ID and a video store membership card.

Looking over these items, you not only learn where to return the bag, but you also learn a fair amount about the bag's owner. Given the evidence in the bag you can make educated guesses about the owner's likes, dislikes, background, and interests. You take the information in front of you and, using your existing knowledge, make judgments about the owner of the bag. We do this all the time with people, regardless of whether we can ever see inside their bookbags.

Reading—good reading—works the same way. The book or article presents you with ideas, facts, and explanations, and you, based on what you know, interpret, analyze, and evaluate that information. If you want to know more about a person you have just met, you do some research: talk to them, talk to their friends, note what book you see them reading next time you pass them at the dining hall, and then sit down and try to figure out what it all adds up to. If you want to understand more about something you are reading you look up words you don't understand, read what others say on the same subject, talk with people about the article, and give yourself some time to figure it out.

In many ways good reading is like good writing. Your initial response to this chapter may be, "I don't need this, I know how to read." Yet, just as you are working to make your writing more focused and effective, you can continually improve and refine your reading skills. You have done this all your life. Certainly you are able to read more complex works now than you could in elementary school. By the time you finish college you will be able to read more complex works than when you started. Just as writing gets easier the more you practice and work at it, reading gets easier the more you read. Some primary sources may be tough to get through at first. The more you work with them, however, the more easily you will understand them—from format to vocabulary to style of writing. It does take work, however.

THE MYTHS ABOUT READING WELL

As with writing, there are several myths about reading that you need to escape to be able to read well at the college level.

Myth 1:   There is one way to read, and all reading is the same.

How can there be more than one way to read? Those funny squiggles on the page form words, the words form sentences, and you know what the writing says. If you think for a moment, you know instinctively the problem with that approach. You read a newspaper differently than you do a novel. You read a scholarly article differently than you do an instruction manual. Just as you put more time and thought into writing a research paper than you do a letter to a friend, different kinds of reading require different levels of attention, thought, reflection, and analysis. A newspaper can be read quickly to find out the happenings of the day. The language is not complex, and you are essentially getting facts without analysis. A Stephen King novel can be read for fun in much the same way. A scholarly article or book, on the other hand, may take much more attention, thought, and reflection. You are not reading it to be entertained or to memorize facts for a test. You are reading it for the ideas, and you have to proceed with care and thoughtfulness in order to evaluate and analyze those ideas.

Myth 2:   Good readers read fast and have to read something only once to understand it fully.

The problem with the first myth points up the weakness in the second. Timed tests, such as the SATs, would make you believe that being able to read fast and to get the general idea of a passage in one reading is the ultimate goal. But good readers—readers who read for ideas, not just for facts—know that they often have to read slowly and deliberately. They know they almost always have to read any complex work two or three times. Again, there is an analogy to writing. The first time you read something is like your first draft. Subsequent readings are like your revisions when you write. Each time you read a piece you will discover new layers of understanding. Not understanding an article on the first reading does not mean you are stupid. It means you are working with complicated ideas and writing that will require you to go back to the work several times to figure out the answers to your questions. Of course, there are times when skimming a passage quickly to see if it is relevant to your work can be useful. Yet, good, in-depth reading takes time and effort. Imagine that someone threw a handful of coins into the bottom of a swimming pool. You probably would not be able to pick them all up on your first trip to the bottom. Instead you have to dive in, get what you can, surface for air, and dive back in again. So it is with reading.

Myth 3: There is a single "correct" meaning or interpretation for any piece you read.

Any thoughtful piece of writing will yield more than one "correct" meaning and interpretation. The data may be clear, but your analysis of those data may differ from your classmate's, your professor's, even the author's. Remember that just because something is in print does not mean that it is true or accurate or that it means exactly what the author says it does. You should feel free to question and challenge the things you read and to seek divergent points of view. Consider if you were told that a friend had been selling illegal drugs on campus, but you did not believe it. You would not simply accept the information without question. You would analyze the information, do your own investigating, think about the credibility of the various sources, and reach your own conclusions.

Myth 4: Writing that is worth reading has to be entertaining or something you can "relate" to.

Good writing always makes anything more enjoyable to read. Yet, not all good ideas come packaged in good writing. Sometimes you have to work through writing that is less than inspiring in order to get to the ideas and data you need. (This should be all the more motivation to make your own writing as compelling and interesting as possible.)

Also, we don't read only what we can "relate" to. If we did, we would never stretch the boundaries of our knowledge and imagination. In fact, this myth should really be turned on its head: Something is worth reading when, by reading it, we learn to "relate" to a new idea, person, place, or theory.

Myth 5: Reading and writing are separate activities.

Good reading and good writing are inextricably woven. A good reader reads with a pen in her hand, taking notes, asking questions, writing down ideas, responding to what she reads as she reads.

Remember that writing helps you think. As you write, you organize your thoughts, make connections, understand problems, define questions—all of which are vital processes to good reading. Conversely, the better you are at reading critically and creatively, the sharper your writing becomes, the better able you are to recognize the strengths and weaknesses in your writing.

A Good Reader's Tools

Reading and note-taking styles can be as individualistic as writing styles. Even so, there are some general ideas that are worth keeping in mind.

First, try to find the articles and book sections that will be useful to you. If you have searched for information using the suggestions and exercises from Chapter Three for finding articles and books and evaluating whether they are what you need, then you should be in fairly good shape by now. (It may help to review, from time to time, the sections in Chapter Three on evaluating sources and finding the books you need.) You may still need to skim a chapter or article—read the abstract, chapter titles, section titles, read the first sentence of paragraphs—to get a sense of the scope and structure of the information.

After you have determined which articles and chapters contain the information you want, you need to slow down to read for content. As a good reader you need to gather the tools you will need to read effectively.

Tools?

Good readers never read alone. Instead, they keep with them a set of mental and physical tools to help them understand and synthesize the information they read.

To be a good reader you need to read with the time and willingness to read a piece more than once. As we've said before, you need to read slowly and carefully to understand a complex piece of writing. That requires giving yourself enough time and having enough patience to do the job right.

To be a good reader you need to read with a willingness to be confused and not panic. Your first reading of a piece may leave you baffled in places and with a fear that you are just not going to understand what the author is saying. Don't fear confusion—embrace it. Because . . .

To be a good reader you need to read with an eagerness to find questions and a desire to answer them. Identify your questions as clearly as you can. Write them down. Also write down what you do understand. Then you have begun to create a structure for comprehending the work, and you can plunge into your next reading intent on finding the answers to those questions.

To be a good reader you need to read with a dictionary nearby. Inevitably good readers, at all levels, come up against words they don't know. It's nothing to be ashamed of. Instead, use the occasion as an opportunity to learn. Increasing your knowledge and vocabulary does not come through memorizing a dictionary. It comes though encountering words you don't know, looking them up, and understanding them in the context of the article. If you run into words you do not understand, don't give up or skip over them; chances are if you have seen them once you will see them again. If a standard dictionary doesn't have the word, or if its definition does not seem to fit the context, use a specialized dictionary like the ones listed in Appendix A. Look up the word and learn.

To be a good reader you need to read with a skeptical, yet open, mind. To read well you have to be an active reader. You have to be ready and willing to challenge ideas and information that raise questions. You have to consider who the authors are and what their possible biases might be. You have to consider whether there are problems in the methodology the authors used, or whether their conclusions are supported by their results. You have to be willing to have your mind changed by compelling evidence and ideas. Don't simply suck up information like a mindless vacuum cleaner. Active reading is like having a conversation with the authors. Respond to what they say. Use your knowledge and read with an active and engaged mind.

To be a good reader you need to know that experts disagree, that theories conflict, that data can be manipulated to make two entirely different points. Very rarely is there a single, correct, and indisputable answer to any question. And, when two or more articles or authors disagree or offer conflicting explanations, you can't simply choose the one you like and ignore the others. On the other hand, you do have to evaluate the different arguments. You have to decide who has the best evidence. You have to find out if other people support one view or the other and why. You have to decide how credible the source is and how influential. (However, keep in mind that many ideas we now accept as the truth initially were given very little support from others and were even seen as crazy or dangerous. Just ask Galileo.)

To be a good reader you need to read with a desire to make connections to other ideas and works. Again, you need to keep thinking as you read. What have other authors said about this subject? Based on your research so far, what did you expect this author to say? How does this information fit into your focus? Does it challenge your focus, or reinforce it? What references does this author use, and do they offer other potential resources for you?

To be a good reader you need to read with pen in hand. Writing helps you think. Writing helps you define questions, find answers, make connections. Writing gets your ideas and questions on paper so you won't forget them. Finally, writing helps you slow down and digest a piece as you read it. Underline passages, put notes in the margins, take notes, do whatever you are comfortable with to write as you read.

TECHNIQUES FOR CREATIVE READING

Note-taking can be a highly idiosyncratic process. Sooner or later everyone develops personal styles of writing abbreviations, highlighting important points, organizing information, and so on. You may already have a system with which you are comfortable and confident. If you do and you see no need to change, fine. On the other hand, there are several options available for taking effective notes, and you may want to experiment with them to see if there are ways of improving your efficiency and effectiveness.

There are essentially two reasons to take notes. First, taking notes can be an effective way to work through a difficult piece of reading. Second, taking notes is a way to gather the information you need for your paper. (Note: Any time you are taking notes you need to be aware of the perils of plagiarism. Don't leave this chapter without reading the section on plagiarism and paraphrasing!)

Taking notes to help you understand something you are reading is a skill you can and should use when you do any kind of academic reading. It is very useful for reading for a research project. It also will help your reading and comprehension skills in all of your classes. If you get into the habit of writing while you read it will help you write better essays, do better on tests, and understand more clearly everything that happens in your classes.

The Double-Entry Journal

There are several methods for using writing to help you read more effectively. The one we find to be most successful is called the "double-entry journal." This is not a journal in the traditional format of a diary. Instead, keeping this journal will help you to understand and analyze what you are reading and to form questions about what isn't clear to you. It is a place for you to make sense out of what you read, to carry on conversations with yourself and with the authors about what you are reading, and to develop ideas you want to explore for writing projects. After you have an idea for a writing project, the reading journal can act as notes, and even as draft sections, for that paper.

The reading journal uses a two-page approach (or you can divide a single page down the middle). You begin by taking notes on the left-hand page of your notebook, leaving the right-hand pages blank. On the left pages you will make comments on the reading as you go along-writing down quotes, paraphrasing, noting your reactions to ideas. You do not have to comment after every paragraph or page, but you shouldn't wait until the end of a book or article to make notes. The right-hand page is for reflection and analysis after you have finished reading. That is the beauty of this system. It allows you to write down ideas and questions as they occur, then to return to those ideas and questions later for evaluation and interpretation.

On the left-hand pages, for example, these are some of the things you might include: notes about important ideas and theories; notes about when the reading changes; notes about when you are surprised or puzzled; questions you have; notes of details (facts, statistics, or examples); notes about how the writing relates to your knowledge, other readings, and your focus; notes about your first impression of the ending of a piece. (There are more specific ideas about what to look for in the following exercise .)

When writing in the journal, try to use full sentences and complete phrases as often as possible. Writing complete sentences will help you form your thoughts fully and help you remember what you were thinking when you refer to your notes. Put page numbers from the book next to the notes to keep the two connected. If you write down a direct quotation, put big quotation marks next to it so you know it isn't a paraphrase. Also, put a large "R" or some other kind of mark, such as brackets surrounding the entire sentence, next to your reactions so you are sure to distinguish them from paraphrases of the author's ideas.

The left-hand pages are for your direct reactions to the reading. The right-hand pages you have left blank are for an analysis drawn from those earlier notes. When you finish a chapter or article, go back and use the facing pages to comment on your original observations and to make connections among your notes. Some readers try to analyze and comment on specific notes on the left-hand side. They try to stop and answer specific questions they might have written or to correct any misreading they might have done. Other readers begin a fast free-write about their reactions and reflections about the reading, using the left-hand- notes as reference and inspiration.

An alternative approach is to divide the left-hand notes as well into direct quotations and paraphrases on the far left side and personal reactions on the other side. This is another way of avoiding confusing your opinions and those of the author. You would still put your interpretations and analysis on the right-hand page after you have finished reading.

Regardless of your approach, here are some of the things you might include on the right-hand notes: What is the main point of this piece? Do you agree or disagree with it? Are the ideas in the piece supported by the data and examples? Where does the reading connect with your knowledge and your other readings? How do the ideas and data in this piece fit within your focus? (Other responses to consider are listed in the following exercise.)

When it comes time to write your research paper—or any other paper—having kept a reading journal will make this much easier. You will be able to use the notes and comments in your journal as a framework and reference for your paper, and you won't have to waste time thumbing through a book for that one passage that will perfectly illustrate your point. It will also help you avoid plagiarism by encouraging you to interpret and rephrase ideas and comments in your own words.

As we said before, the kind of understanding that a double-entry journal can provide will help you with your reading assignments in all of your classes. We both continue to use double-entry journals, as do many professors and many students at both the undergraduate and graduate levels.

A double-entry journal does have one drawback when it comes to writing a research paper. Your notes will be organized by the works you read, not by subject matter, as they might be with a note card system. This means you may find yourself doing some flipping back and forth through your notes to find what you need. We find this is not as significant a problem as you might think because the very process of using a double-entry journal helps you understand and remember a piece so clearly that it is not that hard to find what you need in your notes.

If, however, you need a better sense of organizing these notes, there are several possible solutions, You can go back and make some notecards from the most important points in your journal. You can color-code your note book by subject—more on this in a moment. You can cut apart the pages by subject as you begin to write. (Although some students use this method, we would not recommend it because it destroys your reflections and analysis.)

EXERCISE

The Double-Entry Journal

Find an article or chapter connected to your topic that you feel confident you will be able to read successfully. Using the following questions, create a double-entry journal about the piece. See how your notes alter your understanding of the piece and its connections to other works and ideas.

Now find an article or chapter that has been difficult to read and understand. Again, using the following questions, try using a double-entry journal on this piece. See if the journal helps you work your way through the article and make the connections you need.

Things to look for as you read, to note on the left-hand page:

You see something you didn't see before.

You recognize a pattern—ideas, examples, theories.

The author says something you agree or disagree with.

You find specialized words or phrases that recur or are connected. Or there are words or phrases you don't understand.

The author introduces a new idea or context or perspective.

The author refers to another work with which you are unfamiliar.

Things don't make sense to you—what is the question you would ask the author?

There are statistics or a methodology you don't understand.

The conclusions don't seem justified by the data.

How do the ideas and data connect to other works you have read? Have you seen similar ideas or examples in other articles or books?

Do the ideas or examples support or oppose your thinking on the subject?

Do the authors seem to have a particular bias in their approach or background?

Things to consider after you have read, to note on the right-hand page:

What is the main point of this piece? Do you agree or disagree with it?

Are the ideas in the piece supported by the data and examples?

Where does the reading connect with your knowledge and your other readings?

How do the ideas and data in this piece fit within your focus?

Is there a pattern to the changes you saw?

Does the ending tie things together?

Was a question you had early in the reading answered later on?

Why did you have trouble where you did?

If a double-entry journal doesn't work for you, there are other ways to use writing to help make sense of what you are reading. If you are a person who prefers to mark up the pages of what you are reading—even if it means spending freely to photocopy all the articles you need—you may still find you have trouble with specific parts of an article or chapter or that you are unsure of the overall focus of a piece.

Paragraph Summaries

One way to approach this problem is by paragraph summaries. It works this way: In the margins of what you are reading—or better yet, on a separate sheet of paper—write a one- to two-sentence summary of each paragraph of the piece. Yes, it may take a while, but it will help you in several ways. First, it makes you consider and distill the message in each paragraph. Do not move on until you feel you've come up with a clear summary of that paragraph. You will have to slow down and think about exactly what the author was saying at that point.

Second, if a particular section of the article is giving you trouble, having a clear and succinct sense of what comes before that section may allow you to see the connections necessary to understand the complicated section. (If you are really stuck on one particular section, skipping it to summarize the next section you do understand can be effective. Having surrounded the tough section with clear ideas, you may begin to see what the author would need to bridge that gap.) Also, if you need to talk to someone about the article to find the answers to your questions, having a clearer sense of how to summarize the parts of the piece you do understand will make your questions more focused and effective.

Finally, when you have done this for the whole piece, you will have a sharper sense of the author's overall argument or theory and how it is constructed. This will help you to identify strengths, weaknesses, and the most vital points in the author's work. You will know what sections are most closely connected to your focus and be able to direct your attention there.

Variations on Paragraph Summaries

If you think you are getting the point of individual sections, but you are having trouble with the overall focus of a piece, you might try a variation of summary paragraphs. Instead of writing a summary of every paragraph of the piece, find what you believe to be the key paragraph in each section, or on each page, or find the paragraphs that relate most directly to your research. Again, write a short summary of the main points of each of these key paragraphs. This should begin to give you the scope of the author's focus and a very broad outline as to how it was constructed. If you are still unsure about how those key paragraphs fit together, take a step back and start doing more paragraph summaries until you feel the main point does fall into place.

Sometimes, however, you find yourself facing the opposite problem. You may feel you understand the main point of a piece, but there is an important section that remains unclear. In this instance, try moving from paragraph summaries to sentence paraphrasing. Starting with the paragraph that is giving you trouble, go through it slowly, sentence by sentence—looking up words as necessary—rewriting each sentence in your own words. As you understand each sentence enough to rewrite it, you should begin to understand the paragraph as a whole.

Talking Back to the Author

For some articles or chapters, the problem may not be understanding the ideas, but, instead, figuring out what you think of the ideas and how they fit into your focus. Writing about what you read is one of the best ways to think about and evaluate the information. It forces you to be an active reader and to combine your ideas with those of the author. It helps you identify what questions you still have about an author's work. It helps you think about which elements of the work you find persuasive and memorable and which you find less credible or poorly supported. Like the informal writing you did in Chapter Two to help you find a focus, writing about reading helps you get your thoughts on the page, where you can stand back and study them. As we said at the beginning of the book, writing helps you think. Let it help you think about reading.

As we mentioned before, this is one of the strengths of the writing you do in a double-entry journal after you have finished reading a piece.

Another method of using writing to think about what you have read is to use a kind of focused free-writing similar to what you used in Chapter Two to help find a focus. Just as in Chapter Two, you need to write quickly, without censoring yourself or worrying about moving logically from one thought to the next. You are simply trying to get your ideas on the page so you can get a sense of what you know, what you think about the information you have, and what you still want to understand. The only difference is that this time, instead of writing only from your own knowledge, you are writing about the piece you have just finished reading. Even so, you can use some of the techniques you have used before to get yourself started. For example, make a bold statement about the author's main point and then write your reactions both supporting and attacking it. Or engage the author, on paper, in a fictitious dialogue. Or write a letter to the author explaining what you do and do not like about the article or chapter you have read.

The other technique you can use from Chapter Two is funnel writing. Review the exercise in Chapter Two to remind you how this works. This time, however, you begin with a phrase or sentence about the article you read; then start writing fast, stopping to find the important idea, and write again and so on.

EXERCISE

Free-Writing Revisited

Choose an article you think will be particularly influential to your research project. After reading it, look over your notes carefully for 10 minutes. Now write fast for 10-15 minutes about what you have read. Again, don't worry about making it pretty and don't stop writing. If you come to the end of one thought, move on to the next. Glance at your notes for inspiration if you wish, but don't interrupt the flow of your writing. If you don't know where to start, try one of these techniques:

- Write a letter to the author agreeing with or questioning the main point of the piece.
- Write the main point of the piece at the top of the page and go from there.

- Start your first sentence with, "This article is perfect for my focus because . . ."
- Write an imaginary dialogue with the author. If you are not sure where to begin start by asking the author a question you have after reading the piece.

After you have finished, put the writing aside. Read through it the next day, marking the ideas, examples, and questions that fit your focus or that connect to other articles or ideas. Try this for all of the important articles or chapters you read.

As you write about what you have read you will find not only that you are coming up with your own analysis and interpretations of the material, but you also will find that your writing is connecting it to the ideas and examples in the other books and articles you are reading. Remember that not everything you write about these articles and books will be useful. But, as you review what you have written in free-writing and funnel writing, you will find places where you have made connections, points, arguments, and so on that will be precisely the answers you need to your research questions. Consequently, even before you have begun thinking about writing a draft, your focus will be sharpening, and you will be compiling written material that will make your next step into the draft that much easier.

Gathering And Organizing Information

Using writing to help understand and process reading is a kind of note-taking and writing that you can and should use successfully with anything you read in any class. If you are writing a paper, essay, or proposal involving research, however, you need to take notes for another reason as well: to accumulate the examples, quotations, ideas, theories, and other data you will need to write a well-supported and well-documented paper. This kind of note-taking also requires you to take into account how you organize the information you are gathering so you can find and use it effectively when writing and rewriting your paper.

No matter what method of note-taking you use, always write down the bibliographic information from a source before you begin to read it. If you are using a notebook, write the title, authors, publication, date, and so on at the top of the page. (To know exactly what information you will need, refer to Appendix B on compiling a list of references.) If you are using a note card system, write it down on a separate note card. If you photocopy the article, write it down on the first page of the photocopy. Get it written down first. Get it written down accurately and completely. Make it a habit. That way you don't have to worry about forgetting it later on and consequently either not knowing where the information came from or having to make a trip back to the library just to put together your reference list.

There are, essentially, four approaches to taking notes to gather information: notebooks, note cards, computers, and photocopying. Each has advantages and disadvantages.

Notebooks

Keeping your notes in notebooks offers several significant advantages. First, if you use a technique such as a double-entry journal, you can use the notebook both to help you understand what you are reading and to gather the information you will need for your research paper. That means you have combined two important, but time-consuming, tasks. As we have said, the in-depth understanding gained through a double-entry journal also helps you remember what information will be the most useful to you and where you found it. When you use notebooks, you tend to organize your material by the source. This can be helpful if you remember what kind of information was in a particular article, and you can be certain which notes are from which article or book. Here is one trick you can use to help remember what you have: After you have finished reading and taking notes on a piece, go back and jot down a few important summary words at the beginning of that entry—for example, "study of phobias among high school students" or "study comparing responses to variable and fixed reinforcement schedules" will help jog your memory. Finally, notebooks are physically easy to handle and hard to lose; it is a good idea, however, to get a separate notebook—or three or four—for any lengthy research project.

The disadvantages of notebooks are that you may, when it comes time to write your draft, want to organize your material by subject. This can mean a lot of flipping back and forth through notebooks to find what you need. One way around this is to occasionally go back through your notes and put key words in the margins to indicate which notes are connected to which topics. Also, you may take notes that you later decide you don't need. With a notebook they will still be there, cluttering up the pages; though you can always cross out irrelevant notes you want to ignore.

Note Cards

For some of you, the phrase "research paper" may be synonymous with "note cards." If that is a system you have used before and like using, then stick with it. The obvious advantage of note cards is the ease with which you can arrange and rearrange your information. You can organize information by subject, by source, by type of information (theory, data, interview, etc.), by a rough outline of how you want to organize your paper, by the questions you want to answer. This kind of organization is a kind of writing in itself and, like writing about reading, combines the steps of re-search and writing the draft. The other advantage of note cards is that indi-vidual facts and ideas get separated on individual cards. This is also a disadvantage.

Note cards can separate individual facts and ideas so completely that they lose the context in which the author first used them. Also, because of the size constraints, you can't do much more than write down a paraphrase or fact or quotation on a note card. There is little room to be an activist note-taker, asking questions, making interpretations and connections, and working through a piece of reading using note cards. You have room to gather the information, but less room to process it. Consequently, even if you use note cards to gather information for your paper, you may still want to do some fast writing in notebooks after reading a piece in order to think on the page about what the article or chapter was about. Finally, note cards can be both frustratingly small—it is all too easy to lose that one vital note card just at the wrong time—and frustratingly cumbersome—sometimes carrying about bundles of note cards wrapped in rubber bands is a problem and makes it hard to find quickly the notes you want.

Still, you may want to use note cards. If you do, here are a few things to keep in mind. Use four-by-six cards; give yourself enough room for substan-tive notes. Also, buy enough of them. If you try to cram too much on each note card, you defeat their purpose. For that same reason, you will be less confused later if you use only one side of each note card.

It is usually best to keep one set of cards with only bibliographic mate-rial on them. Then, at the top of each card that you use for a particular source, put the author's name or title of the piece. Also put the page num-ber where you found that note; that way you know where you found the in-formation to use in citations or to find it again. A final tip: On the top of each card, also note the type of information you have put on the card—theory, opinion, fact.

Computers

There are two ways to use a computer for note-taking. If you have a note-book-size computer, you can take it with you to the library and use it as you would notebooks or note cards. This will allow you to create separate files for each source and still be able later to reorganize the information into new files by subject or question or an outline. You can take notes into a computer as if they were on note cards or use it more like a double-entry journal. If you don't have a portable computer, but have easy access to one in your room or a computer lab, you might want to take initial notes in the library on note cards or in a notebook and then do your fast writing about the readings on your computer. This, again, will allow you to take sections of those writings that you intend to use and organize them in a new file for your first draft.

If you are not a fast typist, or if you still don't completely trust using a computer, then stick to pen and paper for your notes. You have enough to think about without having to worry about the technology. Also, computers can be cumbersome and, if you don't keep track of what is in each file, you may find that you can lose a vital piece of information in a computer as easily as you can lose a note card. Finally, remember that computers are machines and that machines ultimately break down. If your computer blacks out on you and turns a month's worth of notes inside of it into electron soup, people all across campus will be able to hear your howls. Do yourself a favor—make frequent printouts of your notes, always make sure you have made backup files, and save your files often.

Photocopying

You're right—technically photocopying isn't note-taking; but it can be an effective complement. Some people do like to arrive at the library with 10 pounds of change to photocopy all the articles they need, take them home, and mark them up. This offers you the advantage of always having available the exact words of the article and the larger context of what comes between the passages you underline. It does not offer you much room to write analysis or interpretation. Again, you may want to move back to a notebook or computer for this. As with notebooks, it also means you will be organizing by source. Even if you don't copy the entire article, you may find it much faster and more accurate to photocopy a page of data, or a page of bibliography, or a chart, than to try to write it all out. Photocopying, although not a substitute for good note-taking, can be an effective supplement.

Color-Coding and Number-Coding

Another aid in organizing material may be color-coding. This system can help you organize both notebooks and note cards. Get a handful of markers in different colors and assign each color to a topic or issue in your focus. For example, you decide that green will represent all of the information you have about the physiological causes of depression. You can go through your notes on a source and put a big green mark next to each note that you have relating to that idea. This will help you locate, at a glance, information you need on a particular topic.

A more monochromatic variation of this is to use numbers to identify the different ideas and then put the corresponding number by the corresponding note.

Whatever system of note-taking you use—and you may end up using a combination of notebooks, note cards, computers, and photocopying—make sure you are consistent and accurate. Find what works for you, then stick with it. And make sure you get the notes right. The system you decide on is only the means to an end. What is important is that you gather the information you need clearly and precisely. In order to do that, you have to have a clear sense of what kind of notes you are taking—the differences between direct quotation, paraphrasing, and summary—and how to avoid the pitfalls of plagiarism.

Quotation, Paraphrasing, And Summary

When you take notes about something you read you use one of four forms: your opinion, direct quotation, paraphrasing, or summary. Your opinions about an article are important and also easy to recognize. You write down your response or interpretation to a piece of information, and that's that. (As we said in the section on the double-entry journal, sometimes it is helpful to put some kind of symbol or brackets next to or around such entries so that later, when you review your notes, it is clear which thoughts belong to you.)

Direct Quotation

Direct quotation can also be useful in a paper. First, it is the most precise way to support your ideas. If someone reading your paper sees your source's exact words backing up your point, it will add strength to that argument or interpretation. Some students wonder if direct quotation and paraphrasing weaken a paper because these forms rely on the ideas of others. On the contrary, used effectively and judiciously, direct quotation and paraphrasing strengthen a paper because they demonstrate to your reader the depth of your knowledge, how you support your ideas, and what theories and data influenced your conclusions.

Direct quotation can, on the other hand, cause problems if you rely on it too heavily. Simply copying one quotation after another from articles and books and then stringing them together in a paper will not give your reader a sense that you have a clear understanding of the material. If you do feel as if your paper is turning into nothing more than a list of quotations, perhaps you need to think more about how you interpret those ideas, what conclusions they suggest to you, and how you can incorporate your thoughts into your writing. Use direct quotations as support and emphasis, not as a substitute for interpretation and analysis.

Second, using direct quotation lets your reader know that there is less possibility that you have manipulated or distorted the ideas or facts from your source.

Third, direct quotation highlights the parts of chapters or articles that you think are important. By shining a spotlight on those passages, you increase their importance in the eyes of your reader. (Yet, as with any theatrical production, if you overuse the spotlight, it loses its effect.)

Finally, direct quotation allows you to vary how your paper sounds. You let voices other than your own writing voice speak, and that makes for more interesting writing. So be on the lookout for direct quotations that not only support your ideas, but that also make their points with effective and interesting writing. If you are in doubt as to whether you would use a passage as direct quotation in your draft, write it down word-for-word anyway. You can always paraphrase or use your own interpretation of it later when you write, but you may not be able to reconstruct the exact quote without a trip back to the library.

Be sure to put big, dark quotation marks around any direct quotations in your notes. Also, as with all note-taking, write down whether this passage is a fact or simply the author's opinion. Anytime you quote directly from a book or article or interview, you must be ready to cite that material—in other words, to show where it came from. We will talk more later in the chapter about some of the formats you can use for this. In the meantime, it is vital to restate that you need to know what source your notes came from and to have all of the bibliographic information for that source written down somewhere.

Paraphrasing

Paraphrasing is every bit as important as direct quotation—in fact, sometimes it is called "indirect quotation"—but it can sometimes be trickier to work with. You probably already know that paraphrasing means putting the ideas or facts of other in your own words. For example, if the original sentence is:

> "Spiro's conclusions were that love for the mother and hatred of the father were, contrary to Malinowski's assertions, stronger in the Trobriand Islands than in the West" (Segall, 1990, p. 36).

to rewrite that as a paraphrase would be:

> Malinowski was contradicted by Spiro, who argued that the Oedipus Complex was, in fact, more powerful in the Trobriand Islands than in the West (Segall, 1990, p. 36).

Or, consider that the original says:

> "But Piaget was not alone in disregarding the sociocultural context; most of the researchers studying cognition in the experimental psychology laboratory, be it concept formation or problem solving, or with the more recent paradigms of artificial intelligence and cognitive science, tend to study the individual in isolation from outside influences" (Segall, 1990, p. 158).

To rewrite that as:

> There is a weakness with laboratory experiments on cognition. Most researchers conducting such studies in the laboratory, don't take into account outside, sociocultural influences on the individual (Segall, 1990, p. 158).

would also be paraphrasing, even though this paraphrase also blends the writer's interpretation into the paragraph. The writer, in paraphrasing, is focusing on the criticisms of laboratory experiments, not on the fact that Piaget could be a target of such criticism. It remains clear, however, that the essential idea of how such experiments don't take into account outside influences on the individual belongs to the original author and not to the writer who is paraphrasing.

You probably also know that paraphrasing is useful for several reasons. First, being able to translate an idea accurately into your own words helps you be certain you have a clear understanding of the idea. Also, the ability to paraphrase accurately will improve the quality of your writing. For example, you like the idea of a particular passage, but it is longer and more detailed than you need for your paper. You can reword and condense it, while keeping the central idea. Or, you may want only part of an idea embedded in a longer passage. By paraphrasing you can extract the idea and rewrite it into complete sentences. Or, as in the preceding example, you may want to blend analysis or interpretation into the information you are rewriting (without, of course, changing the author's meaning). In order to paraphrase effectively, however, you need to significantly rewrite the original quotation. If you are changing only a word or two, you might as well use a direct quotation.

You may also use paraphrasing to reduce unnecessary jargon in a passage or to alter the terms used in a passage to fit your focus. In the same way, you can paraphrase a quotation to make the language fit your writing voice. We haven't talked much yet about the idea of establishing a writing voice; that will come briefly later in this chapter and in more detail in Chapter Five. For now it is important to realize that when you reword a passage, you will be changing the tone, or the voice, of it. This can be useful. There is nothing wrong with paraphrasing an idea so that the language fits more smoothly into your writing. On the other hand, be careful that, as you alter the tone of a passage by rewording it, you do not distort what the author is saying—turning an opinion into a statement of fact, for example. In the same way, you want to make sure that when you paraphrase, you do not omit important ideas that could alter the meaning of the passage. Again, if you are unsure at this point how paraphrasing might change the meaning of a passage, use a direct quotation in your notes. You can decide later when you are writing what form you want for the information.

Finally, paraphrasing will allow you to vary the writing style and tone of your paper. Simply stringing together page after page of direct quotations would get tedious and confusing and give little sense that you truly comprehend the material. Paraphrasing helps you keep the writing lively and interesting.

Paraphrasing, like direct quotation, is using ideas and data from other people. Even though you have put those ideas in your own words, you will need to give credit to the authors with whom the information originated. You will have to cite paraphrased material in your paper. Again, make sure you know which notes came from which article.

EXERCISE

Paraphrasing

Your professor may choose to do this exercise in class. If not, you can do it very effectively with a group of classmates. You can do this exercise in groups, pairs, or individually.

Each group or person chooses the same paragraph from a book or article. Then they rewrite the paragraph in their own words. Try reading the paragraph carefully, then rewriting it without referring to it too often. If you are doing this exercise on your own, try rewriting the paragraph two or three times.

Compare the new, paraphrased paragraphs.

- Which new paragraphs most closely reflect the original text? Why?
- Have the new paragraphs altered the meaning of the original? Why?
- What choices did you make when you were rewriting the paragraph? Why did you make those choices? Did they alter the tone of the passage? How?

Summary

Summary is similar to paraphrasing in that you are rewording the ideas or data of someone else. The difference between paraphrasing and summary is in scope. Paraphrasing information usually means rewording a specific sentence or paragraph or short passage. Summary, instead, deals with larger pieces of information. When you summarize, you are giving the general point, focus, or theme of an article, long paragraph, chapter, or book. You need to use summary when you want to give a quick sense of the overall data, research, or theory but don't need all of the detail.

The idea is to be comprehensive, but brief. For example, to write *This book looks at the ways in which stigmatizing conditions, some visible, some hidden, influence both the public's perception of the individual, and the individual's self-identity and response to public rejection* would be to summarize the book *Stigma* by Erving Goffman (1963). Or, consider if you came across the following paragraph:

> The data tell us that women who are no longer young, regardless of various sexual preferences, are the largest consumers of counselling and therapy from individual clinicians and social agencies. It is hypothesized that this is because women can express their feelings more openly and also feel less

stigmatized than men in seeking and getting professional help. I believe that often therapy is a substitute for friendships. The therapist becomes a paid friend, less threatening than a friend who might require reciprocity or who could prove unpredictable or problematic. The therapist, though costly, must take care of the emotional needs of the client without expecting emotional support in return. There is a safety in this. The therapist relationship may also be terminated without guilt. A friendship relationship which becomes undesired cannot usually be terminated without hurting the other person. There can be expectations that the therapist will change one's life for the better, something that is a great deal to expect of friends or for friends to deliver (Jacobs, 1990, 26).

To write, *Older women may use a therapist as a safe, substitute friend (Jacobs, 1990)* would be a summary of that paragraph.

Summaries, like direct quotations and paraphrases, need to be cited.

EXERCISE

Summary

Using the same groups you did for the paraphrasing exercise, choose a chapter or article with which all of the people are familiar. (If you don't have a single article or chapter that everyone has read, you can pick one from the newspaper.)

Have each person or group write a one-sentence summary of the article or chapter. Again, compare the content, accuracy, and tone of the summaries.

Note-Taking and Voice

As the summary and paraphrasing exercises made clear, changing the way something is written can change its meaning and its tone. The writing tone, sometimes called the writer's "voice," is an important concept to understand and to control. We will talk in Chapter Five about how, while writing and rewriting your paper, you can establish and maintain an engaging and consistent writing voice. You can write in many different voices—advocate, historian, scientist; but part of finding the right voice for a specific paper begins with how you paraphrase and summarize while you take notes.

All you have to work with to alter your writing voice are words, sentences, and paragraphs. The words you choose, the way you structure your sentences and paragraphs, will determine the tone of your writing. For example, every word has a denotation—or its exact meaning—and a connotation—or the mood it sets or ideas it suggests. Although they have the same denotation, there is a definite difference between the tone of the word *spouse* and the tone of *husband* or *wife*. Or think of the difference between *dead* and *expired*, or *loser* and *vanquished*.

The length of a sentence or paragraph and the mix of words also will affect the voice. As you paraphrase or summarize material, be aware of the way in which your rewriting changes the tone from the original. This is not wrong; it is inevitable. Just be sure that the tone of your notes accurately reflects what the author is saying and reflects your reading of the material.

EXERCISE

Note-Taking and Voice

Look again at your paraphrases or summaries and compare them to the way the originals were written.

What is the tone of the original? Write three words that would describe the point of view or the person who wrote it. Now do the same for your version.

How does the rewritten version sound different from the original? Would you describe differently the tone of the original and the tone of what you have rewritten?

How does your choice of words alter the tone of the original? Be specific. How do the structure and the length of your sentences and paragraphs alter the tone?

PLAGIARISM AND HOW TO AVOID IT

Plagiarism. It is the ultimate academic crime. In a world that lives on the exchange of ideas, nothing is worse than to take ideas or writings from someone else and try to pass them off as yours. Consequently, in many colleges, the penalty for plagiarism is at least a failing grade for the paper and often a failing grade for the course or even dismissal from the college. Bad news.

Our experience is that often plagiarism occurs either when someone is lazy or when someone panics. The lazy person wants to get a passing grade without working. The person who panics either procrastinates and then plagiarizes to get the paper in on time, or decides that he can't write a paper good enough to get the grade he needs or wants and plagiarizes to avoid failure. Almost all professors can spot this kind of plagiarism a mile away. Don't be stupid and don't underestimate and insult your professor's intelligence.

If you are reading this book, and if you started work on your paper early and stuck with it, you are probably not a candidate for plagiarism. However, you still might fall into the trap of plagiarizing someone's work, even if you are not intending to cheat. If, by not being careful and accurate with your note-taking, paraphrasing, and citing of sources, you present other people's information as your own, it is still plagiarism. It indicates sloppy work, and it muddies the waters of intellectual communication—the lifeblood of higher education. Plagiarism is wrong, and if you commit it your good intentions do not matter.

The honest and open exchange of ideas is why careful documentation and citations—notes that indicate where material came from—are so vital. It is a matter of integrity and the sharing of knowledge.

When you cite another source you:

- Give credit where it is due.
- Let other people who are interested find the original information you used.
- Give your reader a sense of how you came to your conclusions. In a sense you leave your intellectual footprints for others to follow.

In order to accomplish these goals, however, you have to document and cite everything that you quote, paraphrase, or summarize. It is easy to remember that you have to cite material when you use a direct quotation. When you paraphrase or summarize, however, it can be deceptively easy to put an idea or fact in your paper without acknowledging the source of that information.

A good way to remember when to cite information is to think of it this way: Even if the words are yours, if the idea came from someone else, you are paraphrasing and have to cite.

There is one exception to the preceding rule: common knowledge. This means that, even if the information is new to you, if it is common knowledge to people in general, or to others in the field of your research, you may not have to cite it. A good way to test if information is common knowledge is to ask yourself if it can be found in numerous different sources.

For example, common knowledge can be undisputed dates (John F. Kennedy was elected president in 1960); well-known facts, even if you didn't know them (The corpus collosum connects the two halves of the brain. Sigmund Freud lived in Vienna.); or common terms, facts, and concepts (*fixed interval reinforcement schedule* or *semantic differential*).

The single easiest way to avoid plagiarism is to cite material—quoted, paraphrased, or summarized—that came from any brain other than your own. Even if you occasionally cite material that your professor might consider common knowledge, that is far preferable to plagiarism. There is no quota system for citations; you may use as many as you need.

When in doubt, cite it!

If you are unsure whether to cite some material—for example, you are unsure whether the idea of "blaming the victim" is common knowledge in sociology—ask your professor. Professors would much rather answer a question about citing a source than have to expose and confront a case of plagiarism. Also, if your professor says you do not need to cite something, you are probably safe from plagiarism in that instance.

Always hang on to your notes and your drafts until after you have received your graded paper. People who are lazy or who panic do not take the time and trouble to take notes and write drafts. If you have your notes and drafts and are accused of plagiarism, you can bring those to your professor to show how you did the work and how your thinking evolved as you did your research and writing.

Finally, when you are taking notes and writing your paper, always ask yourself, "Is this my idea, or someone else's?"

CITATION FORMATS

The primary purpose of using citations and bibliographies to document your work is not to catch plagiarists, though it is important to give proper credit to the originator of an idea or study. Instead, as we said, citations and bibliographies help your readers to evaluate your sources and, most important, to be able to follow your intellectual footprints.

By this time you have probably used a reference in a bibliography to find a source for your research. Likewise, someone reading your work will be able to find the same source, if you have cited it properly. The same reader may be able to find other information of interest in your paper and, using your citations and bibliography, be able to track down other sources you used. Citations and bibliographies must be complete and accurate for the free and open communication of information.

There are a number of ways to document the information in your paper; you have probably already used some citation format in writing research papers for other courses. You may be most familiar with using footnotes or endnotes for your citations. Although there is nothing wrong with using these formats, most scholarly writing in the social sciences instead uses some form of internal citation.

Internal citation is, in many ways, a much easier format to use for both the writer and the reader. The essential concept is simple: Every time you use information from another source—quotation, paraphrase, summary, table—you insert parentheses with the name of the author or the title of the piece. (Depending on the format, you also give the date of the publication or the page number where you found the information.) At the end of your paper you have your bibliography or, as it is more often called in these formats, a list of "References" or of "Works Cited." If a reader of your work finds a particular piece of information intriguing, all she has to do is look at the author's name in the parentheses and turn to the list of references at the end of the paper to find all the bibliographic information necessary to locate the source in her library.

The benefit of this format to you as a writer is that citing the information as you write is as easy as dropping in parentheses and the author's name. It is much easier than trying to keep footnotes or endnotes numbered and spaced correctly.

APA Format

You can use several internal citation and reference list forms, each of which is slightly different from each other. In this book we will talk primarily about the American Psychological Association (APA) format and the Modern Languages Association (MLA) format because they are the most widely used in the social sciences. If your professor prefers a different format, find out what it is and where you can find examples of how to use it.

The APA format is used not only in psychology, but often in the other social sciences as well. It works by putting the author's name and the date of publication in the parentheses of the citation. (If you use a direct quotation, you also include the page number where the quotation can be found. You may do this for important paraphrases as well.) This allows readers to know who did the research and how recently it was done, or whether it was done before or after other sources you cite. In APA style you should cite material that is quoted, paraphrased, or summarized. You should also cite material even if you mention the research only in passing. Your readers might still want to locate that source. For specific examples of APA style and how to organize your references and your citations, turn to Appendix B. If you want a much more detailed reference for this format, perhaps because you are thinking of going on to upper-level courses or graduate school or writing for scholarly journals, you need to get the *Publication Manual of the American Psychological Association, Fourth Edition.*

MLA Format

The MLA format is used primarily in the humanities, though some social science journals and professors prefer it. It works essentially the same way as APA style, except that in MLA style you include the author's name and the page number, but not the year of publication, in the parentheses. The references list, called the "List of Works Cited" in MLA style, is slightly different as well. There are some examples of this format in Appendix B. If you need more detail, see the *MLA Handbook for Writers of Research Papers, Fourth Edition.*

Footnotes

Although you probably won't use footnotes to cite material, there may be times when you want to use them for information that is connected to your paper, but to put it in the body of the paper could be confusing or clumsy. In the body of the paper you put a superscript numeral—one slightly above the line of writing—where you want the reader to refer to the note. You put all of the notes, in order by number, on a page at the back of your paper labeled "Footnotes." After the number of the note, you treat the rest of it like an ordinary paragraph. For more on this, see the APA manual.

You've focused, you've researched, you've read. By now you should be collecting enough material to feel confident and knowledgeable about your subject and your ideas and conclusions about that subject. It is time to put it all together. Let's write.

Chapter Five

Putting It All Together

That breeze you are beginning to feel means that there is a draft around somewhere. Before that realization sends a chill from head to toe, you will be pleased to know that you have been working on your draft since Chapter Two. All of the writing you have done—the prewriting you did as you searched for a focus, the note-taking you did as you read sources, the free-writing you did about those sources—will help you construct a strong draft of your paper. (Being able to take the time to do all of this writing should also remind you why, in Chapter Two, we placed so much emphasis on getting an early start on your paper.) There may be some pieces of that earlier writing that you will be able to incorporate almost word for word into your draft. There may be other pieces that give you the idea you need to connect various parts of your focus. And there may be other parts that remind you, with absolute certainty, what you do not want ending up in your draft. It is more important now than ever to have a clear sense of your focus, of what you want your reader to know, and to stick to it.

The obvious next step is figuring out how to combine the writing you have already done with new writing and examples in an organized, engaging, and persuasive draft. That sounds easy, but it may feel a bit over-whelming right now. How are you going to get from the chaos of the mountains of data, theories, and ideas you have in your notes to a paper that makes sense and is interesting to read? There are several approaches you can take to reach this end; but before we get to those, we recommend one last writing exercise.

After weeks of reading other people's ideas, experiments, and conclusions, it may be a little difficult to remember exactly what questions you started out to answer and how this material can be organized to answer them. What you need to do is what Bruce Ballenger, in his wonderful book *The Curious Researcher* (1994), calls "reclaiming your topic." You have to find a way to organize your thoughts about the information you have in front of you and, at the same time, figure out how they will connect to your focus. This will sharpen your sense of the purpose of your paper and suggest more clearly which organizational approach would serve you best in attacking the rest of the draft.

Try the following exercise.

EXERCISE

Reclaiming Your Focus

Start by spending 15 minutes reviewing your notes and rereading key parts of books or articles. Don't worry about remembering it all; simply dive into the information you have. You will remember the most important parts.

Now put your notes away and take out pen and paper.

First,   start writing the story of your research. This is a free-write; don't worry about composing. Simply tell about how your thinking about the project grew and changed. Where did you begin with this research? What were your initial thoughts about the topic? What did you learn that impressed you, reinforced your initial ideas, or changed your mind? If you have conducted an experiment, how did the results confirm or contradict your hypothesis? What is the most interesting idea you have learned? Do you have any unanswered questions? Don't worry if the writing meanders a bit, and don't check your notes. The point of this exercise is to trust that you will remember what is important. Just write fast for at least 10 minutes.

Second,   take a breath, skip a line, and start writing again, this time focusing on the examples, data, case studies, observations, and other details that stand out in your mind. Try to describe them as best you can and to explain why they seem important to your focus. Again, write fast for at least 10 minutes and don't look at your notes.

Third,   write an imaginary dialogue about your topic with another person. Choose a friend, your professor, a researcher whose work you have read—anyone. Start by letting the person ask the most common question people might have about your focus and let it go from there, writing both parts. What would the person ask next? Where might she ask for clarifications? Write fast for at least five minutes.

Finally,   skip a line and write "SO WHAT?" in capital letters. Then try to answer that simple question about your paper. What is the most important idea you want people to understand about this topic or experiment? Try to answer this question until you can do it in two clear and direct sentences.

This exercise helps you sift through what you think about your research. You should be able to get a sense of how your thinking has evolved, what the most important examples are, what questions your readers might want answered. You have done all of it on your terms, with your interpretations and ideas combined with the ideas about which you have been reading. Most important, by answering the "SO WHAT?" question you have essentially restated your focus; you could also see this as your working thesis statement. If it is different from the focus card you have been carrying around, you probably should write a new focus card and put the new one up over your desk or computer as you write.

This writing exercise has done several positive things for you. You have reminded yourself about what was most important or memorable in your research and defined those ideas and issues in your terms. You have redefined your focus. You have begun to establish the writing voice you will use in this paper.

While you let those ideas sink in for a moment and let your writing hand recuperate from the last exercise, it is worth pausing to think about the ideas of audience and writing voice, because they will also influence how you write your draft.

AUDIENCE AND WRITING VOICE

We touched on this idea in Chapter Two, but it is time to think about it again. In writing, an audience is the people who will be reading your work. Defining the audience in college is usually easy; your primary audience will almost always be your professor. A secondary audience might be other students or other professors, but, let's face it, the grade will come from your primary audience. If you went through the list of questions to ask your professor in Chapter Two and have been going to him with questions—and going to class—as you have worked on your project, you should have a fairly good sense by now of who this primary audience is and what he expects.

Keep in mind, however, that your writing audiences will change as you get out of college and that you should always think about who your audiences are and what they expect when you begin a writing task. Are they experts in your field? Or do you need to give them more background? Are you trying to persuade them of a point? Or give them a more objective analysis? Are they your supervisors or employers? Or are you giving instruction to them?

What you determine your audience to be will influence what information you present and how you present that information—or how you choose your writing voice.

Voice, or tone, is important in writing because it lets the reader know what your position is as a writer and how you want the reader to react. A paper arguing against the death penalty will probably not be too successful if it has a light, comic tone. Your purpose, position, and the effect you want to have on the reader will influence what you want the tone to be. You may be accustomed to all academic writing sounding like the textbooks you've read—scrupulously objective, detached, and with little interpretation or argument. Although writing of that kind certainly goes on in colleges, you will soon find that there is also a place in academic writing for passion, persuasion, and even personal experiences. The trick, however, is finding the best writing voice to reflect the purpose of your paper.

If you want to report on events or experiments and let readers draw their own conclusions, you will need a more detached, formal, and objective tone. This means you will probably avoid using personal experiences, writing in the first person, or using a lot of slang. The following example is from a report on a study of brain disfunction related to schizophrenia.

> "Schizophrenia is a disorder characterized by a multiplicity of signs and symptoms, no single one of which is present in all patients. Patients have a mixture of cognitive and emotional disturbances in a variety of functional systems such as perception, language, inferential thinking, and emotional expression and experience" (Andreasen et al., 1994, p. 294).

Notice that the authors use a clear and direct, yet formal and detached writing voice. There is no use of the "first-person" point of view ("I notice . . .") The authors' observations are presented neutrally; we have no sense of whether they thought this situation was good or bad, positive or negative.

On the other hand, if you want to argue a particular point, to persuade the reader to agree with your position, you will need a more involved, perhaps less formal and more passionate tone. The first-person voice ("I believe. . .") may be appropriate, as might personal experiences. For example, Tim was writing a paper about discipline in the classroom:

> "As an educator I had worked to create a disciplined classroom using punishment as the main tool to achieve control. I have, in the past, met with a great deal of success, in so much as I had established a quiet and reasonably respectful environment in the classroom. The question I now face is, at what cost to the students was this control achieved?"

In this passage, Tim's experiences as a teacher are useful information he can draw on. They also give us, as readers, a clearer sense of the motivations and goals guiding his research.

In the same way, a paper using personal experience may have a different tone than one relying more on interviews with others.

A paper directed at experts in the field may have a very different tone than one written for a general audience. A paper for experts can use specialized language without having either to explain the words or to worry about losing the readers. For example:

> "The core of ordinary belief/desire psychology has been isolated and made more rigorous in normative decision theory. The confidence we have in the contents of our beliefs and the intensity of our desires can be used in ideal cases to measure subjective probability and utility" (Manktelow & Over, 1990, p. 161).

A paper for a more general audience will have to avoid too much specialized language, explain the terms that are there, and may also have to provide more background for the readers about the issues involved. At the same time, you do not want to talk down to an intelligent, general audience. For example:

> "The researchers . . . explained that in our culture, as in most, aggression is seen as more typical of males than females. In other words, it is a masculine-typed behavior" (Hock, 1992, p. 92).

Choosing Your Voice

Although a particular writing voice may be more appropriate for your topic and your approach, that doesn't mean there is only a single voice available to you. Just as you can alter the meaning of a word you speak by changing your tone of voice, you can alter your writing voice to change the way the reader reacts to the same information.

Consider, for example, nursery rhymes.
Nursery rhymes?
Quickly write down these nursery rhymes:

"Three Blind Mice"
"Humpty Dumpty"

Now read the following examples.

Three rodents with impaired ocular implements
Three rodents with impaired ocular implements
Note their rapid perambulations
Note their rapid perambulations
In totality they pursued the agriculturalist's spouse
Who amputated their hind appendages with a carving utensil
Have you ever witnessed such a phenomenon in your existence
As three rodents with impaired ocular implements?

The victim, one Humpty Dumpty, was, at the point in time of the accident, seated atop a free-standing structure at the scene of the aforementioned accident.

Mr. Dumpty's rapid, unplanned descent from the structure resulted in violent interface with the ground.

Elements of the monarchical authority's cavalry and infantry divisions were unable to restore the victim to predescent, preground-interface status.

The events in the rhymes are essentially the same; yet they sound very different.

How did we alter the writing voice to make it sound at times like a police report and at other times like a scientific report?

Look at the differences in the words we chose-"ocular implements" instead of "eyes," "perambulations" instead of "run," "restore" instead of "put."

Also look at the differences in sentence length. The second line of our version of "Humpty Dumpty" has 15 words instead of the traditional six. This long and rambling sentence robs the climax of any action or drama. (Although not applicable for nursery rhymes, varying paragraph length can have a similar effect on the writing voice.)

EXERCISE

Writing Voice: Nursery Rhymes

Try one of your own. Choose your favorite nursery rhyme and turn it into contemporary slang. Now rewrite it as scientific jargon. Notice how different words create different moods. Compare your examples with those of fellow students and see how both words and sentence length change the writing voice.

Of course, you are not writing nursery rhymes. Yet, these examples should remind you that you have numerous options in terms of writing voice. Choose your voice and your words with care. Make sure they sound appropriate and consistent for your paper.

Tone, or voice, is an elusive and sometimes troublesome concept. But the wrong tone for your paper can mislead or confuse your readers and weaken your paper. The point is to be aware that you have choices and that the choices you make will affect your final paper. Also, after you establish a tone in your writing, try to keep it consistent.

EXERCISE

Writing Voice: A Checklist

This is a quickie, a pause to help you clarify your thoughts about the writing voice you choose.

First, read the assignment for this paper again. Then think about your audience.

From the following list of words, choose the ones that best describe what you think the most effective and appropriate writing voice will be.

Objective/Subjective

Formal/Informal

First person/Anonymous author

Persuasion

Documentation

Explanation

Analysis

Evaluation

Review

Critique

Active Voice

Another component of voice to consider is "active" voice. Active voice means it is clear in a sentence who is doing the action. The opposite of active voice is "passive" voice, in which the action seems to happen by itself.

For example, a sentence in passive voice—"Shouts were heard in the hall."—gives no sense as to whether the shouters were children, adults, politicians, or what.

To write the sentence in active voice—"The students shouted in the hall."—is more precise and more confident. ("The rebellious psychology students shouted insults at the administrators standing in the hall" would be even more precise, and stronger.) If you are told not to use the pronoun "I" in your writing you can always use active voice by writing, for example, "This researcher found . . ."

Use the active voice whenever possible. It is stronger and avoids confusion. Make sure your writing tells who is saying, who is acting, who believes, who argues, who contradicts, who concludes. Don't hide behind the murkiness of passive voice.

Avoiding Sexist Language

Finally, there is the question of sexist language. Words have power, and to always refer to researchers, professors, and all other people as "he" or "him" reinforces the view that only the male half of the world can fulfill those roles. (In fact, there is research [Hyde, 1984; Moulton, Robinson, & Elias, 1978] that indicates that when people use male-only terms and pronouns, others usually envision only men in those roles.) The bias is subtle and usually unintentional; but to refer to only "man" or "mankind" or "he" or "congressman" will give your writing a particular slant.

The *Publication Manual of the American Psychological Association* also recommends that you avoid sexist language in your writing. The suggestions we offer are consistent with APA style. For a more detailed listing of the APA's recommendations, you should consult the manual.

There are four fairly simple ways to avoid sexist language in your writing.

First, the best idea is often to look for a different word. Use *humanity* instead of *man, people* or *humankind* instead of *mankind*. Also, don't assume that you can use male-only names for jobs that have been traditionally dominated by men. Use *representative* instead of *congressman* or *police officer* instead of *policeman*. Use *worker* instead of *workman*.

Second, if you find you are having trouble deciding whether to use *he* or *she* (because English lacks a good, gender-neutral pronoun to replace them), try using a more specific term instead of the pronoun. For example, rather than write, "He must be aware of the margin of error," you could write, "The researcher must be aware of the margin of error."

Also, you can avoid the problems of pronouns by making sentences plural. We have used this technique frequently in this book. For example, instead of writing, "The student should plan to have his reading done by Tuesday," you could write, "The students should plan to have their reading done by Tuesday."

Finally, if you can't use a more specific word or make the sentence plural, there are three other approaches you can use to avoid using male-only pronouns. You can alternate using *he* and *she* with each example or each paragraph. (This is an approach we use in this book.) Or you can write "he or she" or "her or his"; this can become awkward to read, however, if you use it too often. Some professors and scholarly journals recommend you use *he/she* or *s/he*. (Before using this approach, check with your professor. Some do not view *s/he* as a real word and try to discourage its use. The APA also does not recommend using *s/he*.)

Most important, avoid stereotypical thinking. Women can be excellent physicians and researchers, and men can be excellent day-care workers and single parents. Open your mind and your writing to the possibilities.

ORGANIZING THE DRAFT

By now you should have a clear sense of the focus of your piece, what you want the reader to know, and what are the most important ideas and examples with which you will be working. This is the point at which many writers find it helpful to come up with some kind of an outline to help them get a clear sense of the overall shape they will give to the paper.

As you consider the form your paper will take, you might want to think about what overall organizational strategy you want to use. Not every paper should be written in the same way, and it can be helpful to think about what kind of framework you want to build your paper around. (Some kinds of writing-such as experimental reports-require a particular overall structure, which we describe in Appendix C. Within each section of the report, however, there are still organizational decisions you must make.) What you need to think about are the main point of your paper, what information you will be using, and what will be the most engaging and effective way of presenting that.

Choosing a Structure

Imagine for a moment that your larger topic for your paper was the homeless. Depending on your specific focus, the information you have, and what position you are taking as the author, there are several frameworks you could employ.

- If you have a particularly strong and compelling case study you plan on using to illustrate how community mental-health workers try to work with some homeless people, you might want to begin with that **specific** example and move on to a discussion of the issue in **general**. (Or, you could reverse it and begin by outlining the issue in **general** and then move on to how it can be illustrated in this **specific** case study.)

- If your focus concerns deinstitutionalizing mental-health patients and how that contributed to the problem of homelessness, you could begin by discussing how deinstitutionalization as a **cause** contributed to the **effect** of homelessness. (Or, again, you could invert this framework and begin by detailing the **effect** of homelessness and then trace it back to deinstitutionalization as a **cause**.)

- If you are focusing on whether close family associations have an impact on whether a person becomes homeless, you could essentially construct your paper so it followed the course of your research, beginning with that **question** and then showing how that material led you to your **answer** or conclusion. (If the **question** you begin your paper with is stated in the form of a **problem**—for example, "Why aren't particular drug-treatment programs more effective when dealing with a certain population of the homeless?"—the **answer** you conclude with may also have to contain suggestions for a **solution**.)

- Your focus may have led you to research that is sharply divided on an issue. For example, if your focus concerns what kinds of housing options are most effective in helping homeless people stay off the streets, you may find that there is a certain level of **controversy** about the subject. Use this controversy as a framework. You can do it by first presenting one side's **views** on all of the issues, and then the opponents' **views.** Or you can organize your paper by the issues involved and, for each issue, detail the **opposing opinions.**

- If your focus concerns studying different community mental-health approaches toward the homeless in two different cities or countries, you might want to use a **comparison** structure. Again, you can organize this by presenting each community and then looking at their similarities and differences. Or you can organize your paper by the similarities and differences, using the two communities as examples.
- If you want to focus on how theories of the best way to help the homeless have changed in the last 15 years, you may want to organize your paper by doing a **chronology of the research.** You would begin with the earliest ideas and studies and then chronicle how the thinking of researchers evolved in subsequent studies.

Of course, these are only broad ideas for the framework you choose for your paper. They are not mutually exclusive. Combining two approaches, such as specific-to-general and comparison, may work best for you.

The best structure for your paper is the one that will help you answer this question: "What do I want the reader to know when she is finished reading?" It will also allow you to incorporate your own analysis, opinions, and conclusions into the paper. If you are focusing on a controversy, you need to evaluate the opinions of the various sides. If you are focusing on a problem, you need to consider presenting a solution and persuading your reader of its effectiveness. If you are comparing two different approaches, you need to analyze why one may be more useful than the other.

Creating an Outline

You probably have a great deal of the structure of your paper blocked out in your head. The advantage of putting it on paper in some kind of outline is the same as having a road map along with you on a trip you have taken once before. You are reasonably certain you know how to get there, but it won't hurt to have a map to glance at now and then just in case. Also, should you happen to take the wrong turn or run into a traffic jam, you can use the map to find a way around it.

There are as many ways to create an outline as there are writers. You don't have to use the formal outline format you may have learned in high school (unless that is the system that works best for you); you can organize by key words, or by sentences, or by important studies, or a combination of these. The point of creating an outline is to block out the order in which you want to present your primary ideas. Each idea or concept should lead logically to the next until you reach your conclusions at the end of the paper. An outline should remind you which major examples you will use to support those ideas and which explanations and conclusions you will present at each stage of the paper.

You can start by taking the key ideas from your "Reclaiming Your Focus" exercise and organizing them. Or you may want to review your notes, find the way you have written the ideas there, and write out a full sentence or phrase for each idea. You may want to take the key questions from the dialogue you wrote and organize those in a logical order. Or, if you have been using note cards, you can shuffle them around until you get them in the order you like.

After you have outlined the essential ideas of your paper, fill in beneath each idea the other theories, opinions, and examples you will need to use to explain that idea. Then you can organize these smaller elements until they lead logically to the next larger idea or concept.

Think of this again as a road map, and each idea as a town along your route. Your reader will be stopping at each of these towns, and you need to think about what you want your reader to see at each stop before moving on to the next town. At the end of the paper, the final destination, the reason for the reader's journey should be absolutely clear.

Outlines can be useful. Still, be ready to alter them if, as you write your draft, other ideas or examples or conclusions come to mind. Remember that good road maps have more than one road.

Leading Your Reader In

Of course, you have to give your reader a good reason to start this trip. As you move from your outline to writing your draft, you are faced with the decision of where and how to begin. What should you use for your introduction, also called the "lead"? Some writers like to work on their lead first, before doing the remainder of an outline. They believe that what they write in the first paragraph or two will so influence the shape of the rest of the paper that they have to get the lead set first. Other writers prefer to know what shape the paper will take before deciding what will be the most effective lead. The point at which you start writing your lead is up to you. Either way, it is a vital part of your paper that fills several purposes.

A good lead, whether it is one paragraph or five, should, of course, give you a sense of the focus of the paper. It should let you know not only the subject of the paper, but also the scope of your focus. Which elements of this issue are you going to address? What points are you going to try to make? What are you going to prove? This may be contained in a key thesis statement that is only a sentence or two long.

For example:

"Academics and others have long debated whether capital punishment is effective in deterring murder. In this analysis we (1) assess the state of knowledge regarding murder, capital punishment and deterrence; (2) explicate the need to consider different types of homicide in examining the deterrence question; and (3) examine the possible deterrent effect of capital punishment on lethal assaults against police" (Bailey & Peterson, 1994, p. 53).

We know what the overall subject of this paper is and what the writers' specific focus will be.

A good lead will also give you a sense of the tone, the writing voice, of the piece. It will tip you off as to whether the paper will try to persuade, or analyze, or report. For example, Jennifer's paper on homeless children begins this way:

> "Our wealthy America is robbed of its riches when we see the devastating effect of homelessness on our nation's children."

This paper is clearly going to try to persuade us that the effect of homelessness on children is a crisis of nationwide proportions.

Last, but perhaps most important, a good lead grabs the reader's attention. Your professor may have to read your paper, but that won't always be the case with the audiences for whom you write. The more engaging your lead is, the better the chances are that your reader will continue to read the rest of the piece (and even your professor will find it more interesting and compelling). Even in research reports, an engaging introduction will entice more people to read the rest of your study.

After you catch the reader's attention, you can be sure that the reader will continue reading and get to the larger ideas and background. Think about movies your have seen, such as *Jurassic Park* or *Raiders of the Lost Ark.* These movies begin with action and details, without worrying yet about filling you in on all of the background. You watch Indiana Jones try to steal the golden idol for 10 minutes before you even know his name; yet few people walk out on the movie in those first 10 minutes.

You may not have angry dinosaurs or rolling boulders to use in your lead. Still, you probably do have detailed examples, ideas, or images you can use to capture your reader's interest. Very often a more precise, detailed statement lead is more effective than a set of broad, general statements. For example, Mary began a chapter for a book this way:

> "Negative and patronizing societal attitudes have long made people with disabilities the object of oppression and discrimination in every facet of life" (Brydon-Miller, 1993, p. 125).

You could use a detailed quote or good example to lead a piece if it gives the reader a specific image, fact, or person to hang the later ideas on. Ruth used this quotation to begin her paper on the development of Alzheimer's disease:

> "Alzheimer's Disease is worse than death. It leaves bone and flesh intact while it erases judgment and memory. I could live with death. Death is a part of the cycle of life. It's like spring, the end of winter. But this disease—it's unnatural. It's the end of hope" (Cohen & Eisdorfen, 1983, p. 60).

In the same way a strong, detailed example can put your issue in clear and understandable human terms that will intrigue and interest your reader. Josef Stalin is reported to have said, "Ten million deaths are a statistic; one death is a tragedy." If you want your readers to think about the human element of a larger problem you might consider a lead such as the one Alexia used in her paper about the psychological effects on family members who consider the possibility of euthanasia for a loved one:

> "Nancy Cruzan, now thirty-two, has done nothing for the past seven years. She has not hugged her mother or gazed out the window or played with her nieces. She has neither laughed nor wept, her parents say, nor spoken a word. Since her car crashed on an icy night, she has lain so still for so long that her hands have curled into claws; nurses wedge napkins under her fingers to prevent the nails from piercing her wrists" (Gibbs, 1990, p. 62).

There are other approaches you can use for leads. You can present a problem. You can outline the opposing views about an issue. Or you can try an approach that combines several of these ideas. You may need to try several different leads before you find the one that reflects the focus and tone of your paper.

EXERCISE

Writing Leads

Go through your notes and try to find three strong quotations, examples, statements, or facts that you could use as a lead. Remember that you want your lead to grab the reader's attention and to give a sense of your focus and the tone of the paper.

Write at least three leads using what you gathered.

Let some friends or classmates read those leads. Don't tell the readers your focus. After they read the leads ask your readers to tell you what they think the paper is going to be about and what the tone of the paper is going to be. If the answers you get are fairly accurate, then ask the readers which lead is the most effective, which makes them want to read more.

If none of your first three leads seems to be working, then you may have to try more until you get one that gets your readers' attention, gives a sense of your focus, and gives a sense of your tone or writing voice.

COMPLETING THE DRAFT

You now have everything in place that you need to begin working your way through your draft. After your lead you will begin to present your ideas, checking your outline from time to time to make sure you are following the right road. You will want to explain each idea or concept clearly, and then provide the examples or quotations or data that support or refute that idea and explain why they support or refute it.

A good rule of thumb to keep in mind is that every idea or concept needs an example illustrating it and an explanation of the reasons behind it. There are exceptions, of course, but it is a good general guideline to follow.

As you find in your notes the examples and quotations to support and illustrate your ideas, you need to think about how to use them most effectively in your writing. Some students, unfortunately, believe that writing a research paper or report is simply a matter of stringing quotations together. The result of this approach is a series of long quotations strung together without a clear sense of context or interpretation. It makes for a paper that is both boring and clumsy.

As we mentioned in Chapter Four, there are different advantages in paraphrasing a source, summarizing it, and quoting it directly. When it comes to incorporating those elements into your writing, however, you can use them all. A good mix of these elements will provide your writing with the variety it needs to be consistently interesting. So, if you find you have bunched a number of direct quotations together, try paraphrasing some of them in order to create a better mix and to give a clearer sense of your understanding of the material. If you find a particularly effective or precise quotation, don't be afraid to use it.

Even with direct quotations, you don't have to quote the full paragraph or sentence; you can simply use the part that illustrates and supports your idea. (Be careful, however, if you use a partial quotation, to be faithful to the overall context of the passage. You do not want to distort an author's views.)

Along with the information from your sources, you should be blending your analysis and commentary. If you have used a double-entry journal and completed the "Reclaiming Your Focus" exercise from earlier in this chapter you should have the examples, paraphrases, and quotations to work with, as well as a sense of your opinions and interpretations of those sources.

Look at the following example from Kevin's introduction to his paper on the psychology of college drinking:

> "I freely admit that I am part of the 86% of students at the University of New Hampshire who drink. In fact, it is for this very reason that I have chosen to write about why college students drink. When I began exploring this topic, I was amazed at the statistics I read. In 1991, Surgeon General Antonia C. Novello reported that college students 'consume more than 430 million gallons of alcoholic beverages a year and spend about $4.2 billion on alcohol annually' (Magner, 1991, A32). To put it in simple terms, this statistic shows that college students now spend more money on alcohol than they do on textbooks (Cannady, 1994). It was statistics such as these

that gave me a place to begin my research and helped me define the size of the alcohol problem on college campuses."

Notice the combination of statistics, direct quotation, paraphrasing, and personal analysis that Kevin works into that paragraph. He does not simply list statistics and facts or use the quotation without putting it in a larger context. Instead, he makes the connections between the ideas and facts he has found in different sources and then gives a clear sense of how those influenced his thinking.

Of course, the most important thing to do in your writing is to stick to your focus and make sure that your ideas are clearly explained and illustrated. Yet, in terms of writing well, providing variety in the way you use your material comes in a close second. Not only should you blend information and analysis, but you should vary the sources you use as well. Just as in your research you didn't read only one article, when you are writing you should incorporate more than one author's views or study. Use different sources, use different kinds of examples. If it is appropriate, use a mix of both statistics and human examples or case studies.

To write well requires flexibility. Having an outline can be very useful. Still, you should be ready to change the outline or to shift ideas or examples around if, as you write, you find that makes better sense to you. You may find, for example, that halfway through a first draft you find a quotation or example that would make a stronger and more appropriate lead. Go ahead and make the change even if it requires shifting other material. Use your instincts. You want the writing to be clear, persuasive, and engaging. You want your reader to be as interested in the material as you are and to understand exactly what you mean every step of the way.

ENDINGS

There is a huge difference between a paper that has a satisfying ending and one that simply stops. Your ending is the last idea your reader will take away from your paper. Consequently, you want an ending that not only completes your focus, but also provokes continued thought about the subject.

Endings can feel difficult to write. Unlike writing your lead, where you have unlimited possibilities about how to start your paper, by the time you get to the end, you have fewer options because you need to be consistent with the rest of your paper. If your outline hasn't given you a clear sense of what you want your final idea to be, there are a few approaches to consider—and one to avoid.

You may have been told, in the past, that an ending to an academic paper should summarize what you have said. If you think about it, however, you can see why this will probably not provide you with an effective ending. Consider what you would think about a movie that stopped five minutes from the end to review what you had already seen and then ended. Simply repeating what you have already said is not good enough. There are better alternatives.

The structure you have chosen for your paper may influence what you do with the ending. If your paper is constructed around the examination of a particular problem, a possible ending might consist of solutions to that problem, both your ideas and those you have gathered during your re- search. So, for example, if you had been examining the inadequacy of drug- treatment programs for a certain population of the homeless, your ending could contain possible solutions to that problem.

Or, if you have structured your paper around a specific case study or experiment, you might want your ending to address the broader implica- tions posed by your analysis. A formal research report has a specific section for this kind of conclusion. (For more on this, see Appendix C.) To return to our earlier examples of papers about homelessness, a paper detailing a specific homeless person's dealings with the community mental-health sys- tem might end by exploring what this case study implies about such men- tal-health systems in general.

In the same way, if your paper's structure is designed around a specific question, your ending should clearly give a sense of what you see as the an- swer to that question.

Although you want to avoid a summary ending, you may, in fact, want to use your ending to sum up. Let's say your paper has presented several differing views about an issue or has discussed several different experi- ments. Your ending, then, might call for you to evaluate the various opin- ions and reach your own conclusions about the issue. You are not simply rehashing what you have already said; instead, you are presenting a final synthesis of ideas based on information you have gathered. For example, if your paper were about the debate over what kinds of housing options help the homeless most effectively, then your ending should evaluate the differ- ent opinions and reach a conclusion of your own.

The writing voice you choose may also influence how you end your paper. A paper in which you are assuming a more activist voice may need an ending that is a call to action—an attempt to persuade your reader to advocate the same ideas as your paper does.

Finally, you may feel that, by the end of the paper, you have presented all of the ideas needed to understand your focus and explained all of the reasons behind those ideas. Yet, somehow, the paper doesn't seem com- plete. Then you should consider approaching the ending much as you did the lead. Is there a final example, or image, or quotation with which you can end the paper? You aren't presenting any new ideas, but you are giving the reader one final image or thought to keep in mind. For example, a paper examining how close family relations affect homeless people could end with an example of one person who had remained attached to his family.

REWRITING AND REVISING THE DRAFT

After you've finished the first draft, sit back, take a deep breath, and savor your accomplishment. (Even better, take a break. Take a day or two if you can. Give yourself some time away from the draft to recharge your batteries and gain some perspective on the project.)

Welcome back. It is time to get on with the process of rewriting and revising. Revising is essential to good writing. Rare is the writer who writes perfectly in one try. So don't see this as some kind of punishment. You have not failed if your first draft isn't perfect. The first draft is just another step in the process. Now that it is written, what you need to do is to step back from that draft and examine it carefully. You want to make sure that you are being clear, logical, and consistent in ideas and voice, and that you do not have any excess baggage getting in the way of your focus.

Revising is usually more than just tinkering with words and punctuation. You may have to substantially rewrite parts of the paper, add new sections, cut back on others. At times it may be hard work. Yet, virtually all good writers, regardless of their field's, give themselves time to rewrite and revise substantially after the first draft.

Revision for Ideas and Structure

Often the hardest part of revision is being able to think about your paper in any form other than the one you have completed in the first draft. In fact, at this point, you may have been involved with this project for so long that it is getting hard for you to have a clear sense of what is good in the paper at all. Yet, successful revision requires "re-vision"—in other words, trying to see your draft with fresh eyes.

There are several exercises you can try, however, to give you a fresh sense of what you have written and a clearer idea of the draft's strengths and weaknesses. We would not expect you to do all of these exercises every time you write a paper. We *would* expect you to try each of them at least once and to find which ones work best to help you see your draft with fresh eyes and find and correct its flaws.

At this point, you want to concentrate on whether the ideas in your paper are explained and illustrated clearly and on whether the structure of your paper is effective at presenting those ideas in a logical, comprehensible way.

EXERCISE

Cut and Paste

You might want to start the revision process with a little radical surgery. This exercise might seem both a little scary and a little crazy at first. But be courageous and take our word for it; it works to help you see your draft with fresh eyes.

Make an *extra* printout or photocopy of your first draft. Then cut it apart, paragraph by paragraph. Finally, shuffle the paragraphs around so that the original draft is out of order (this is why you want to do this with an extra copy).

Now, clear off a table or desk and begin to go through the stack of paragraphs. The first thing you are looking for is the "key" paragraph. Which paragraph is absolutely essential to understanding your focus—your paper couldn't do without it?

After you have found the "key" paragraph, look through the others. Put into one pile any that have strong connections to the "key" paragraph, that help you understand it more clearly. These can be explanations, examples, or connected ideas. Put into a second pile any paragraphs that seem less strongly connected. (Be hard on yourself. You can always salvage paragraphs from the second pile later.)

Turn to the pile of essential paragraphs and play around. Try different paragraphs as the lead. Organize the ideas in different ways. Try to give yourself a sense of the possibilities. You may find a new structure or new lead that you like better than the first draft. Or you may find that you liked the way you had it the first time.

After you begin to settle on an order you like, start taping the paragraphs together. Make sure to note where you need to add information, analysis, or transitions.

Now that you have a "re-vision" of your work, you can begin rewriting it.

Getting Help From Others

If you can arrange it, one of the best ways to get a "re-vision" of your draft is to find a fresh pair of eyes to read it. As we mentioned in Chapter Two, getting someone else to help you think about your work can be invaluable. It is particularly helpful at this point in the writing process when you may have difficulty seeing your own work objectively.

Try the following exercise with a classmate. It takes some time to do. But because it gives you a chance both to analyze your own draft and to see how another person would analyze it, it is extremely effective in giving you a sense of your draft's strengths and weaknesses. Just remember that when you read someone else's work, try to be both honest and constructive.

EXERCISE

The Writer/Reader Analysis

After you have written a first draft of a paper, it is often difficult to stand back from it and see essential problems with the ideas and organization.

This exercise not only lets you go through your draft carefully to test it for holes and inconsistencies, but it also gives you a reader's initial perspectives on your draft. If your professor does not have you do this exercise in class, you can do it with a classmate in an hour or so.

First, number the paragraphs in your paper (a big number in the margins, please).

Then take out a fresh sheet of paper and put the number "1" at the top.

For each paragraph, put a number on the blank sheet of paper and answer these three questions:

1. What does the paragraph say? (What is a one- or two- sentence summary of the central idea of the paragraph?)
2. What purpose does the paragraph serve in the paper? (For example: It introduces a new idea, or it illustrates an idea with examples, it explains the reasons behind a writer's conclusions, it provides a transition between ideas.)
3. What do you want the reader to be thinking about at this point in the paper?

After you have finished with each paragraph and reached the end of the paper, answer these two questions:

1. What is the main point of this paper?
2. When a reader is finished with the paper, what do you want her to know or to be thinking about?

After you have done this with your draft, trade drafts with a classmate (just the drafts, not the pages with the answers to the preceding questions).

Your classmate reading the draft now takes a sheet of paper—puts her name on it—and puts a number "1" at the top. She now reads the draft, answering the same questions that you, the writer, did, but with a reader's perspective. (And you do the same with her paper.)

1. What does the paragraph say?
2. What purpose does the paragraph seem to serve in the paper?
3. What are you, as a reader, thinking about at this point in the paper?

At the end, the reader then answers:

1. What was the main point of this paper?
2. What did you learn from it? What did it leave you thinking about?

The draft and the reader's comments then are returned to you, the writer.

This exercise will help you check your organization, the focus of each paragraph, the role of each paragraph, and the overall effect of the piece.

You can then check these conclusions against the reactions and ideas of a reader. If you can, you should give yourself time to talk about the comments with your classmate, in case any of them need further explanation or clarification.

As we mentioned in Chapter Two, working with another person during a research project can be helpful at every stage. You can help each other refine your focuses, you can help each other find the best sources for your research, you can help each other understand complex ideas and writing. After you have completed a full draft of your paper, working with someone else can be particularly valuable—as we illustrated with the Writer/Reader Analysis.

Another way to help each other at this stage is to do a more traditional writers' workshop. Again, this is a way to get a sense of how other people respond to your work. Do they understand all the ideas? Do they have questions? Are there suggestions they can make to help you improve your paper?

As we said earlier, the key concepts of effective collaboration, and effective workshops, are respect and constructiveness. The idea is to help out each other, not to rip apart each other's work. You can do workshops in class, outside of class with a single classmate, or with several classmates. The more perspectives you can get on your draft, the more options you will have to choose from when you revise.

There are several important guidelines to keep in mind when reading another person's draft.

First,	start with the largest comments and then get more detailed. In other words, if there is a problem with the focus, don't start by mentioning misspelled words.
Second,	the place for detail is in your comments. If you like the person's examples, show which ones you like and explain why. If you have questions about the focus, explain them as clearly as possible. If you have suggestions for a better ending, explain exactly what those suggestions are. These kinds of detailed comments require reading carefully and making clear comments.
Third,	make sure to mention the good stuff. It is as important to know what is working and what you, the writer, should not change as it is to know what the problems are.
Fourth,	couple every criticism with a suggestion. Do not simply say you do not like the lead or a particular paragraph; instead, explain the problem you have with it and then suggest how the writer might improve it.

As the writer of a draft, when you hear what other people have to say in a workshop, you need to keep two things in mind.

First,	don't get defensive. This is not always easy, but listen to what your readers have to say, take notes, and ask them to explain their comments if you are not sure what they mean.

Second,   after you listen carefully to what your readers say, it is up to *you* to decide if you want to incorporate those changes. It is still your paper. Listen to the comments, consider them, and then use the ones that make sense to you, given what you want your paper to say.

EXERCISE

Workshop Questions

If you are not sure how to approach reading and commenting on another person's draft, here are some questions to keep in mind as you read the paper and some questions to answer after you have finished reading.

As you are reading:

- Does the introduction give you a sense of what the paper is going to be about? Do you know if the writer is going to take a particular position on this topic? Do you want to read more?
- Note when you are surprised or intrigued by ideas or examples that you read.
- Write down questions that occur to you and any examples or theories you either don't understand or don't know why they were included in the paper.
- Note any place where you feel an example would help to explain or illustrate an idea.
- Are there clear transitions from one idea to the next? Is the writing too wordy or too choppy?
- Is the ending satisfying?

When you have finished reading:

- Summarize the main point of the paper.
- Did your ideas about the subject change as you read the paper?
- Are there any ideas or theories you would like the writer to explore or explain in more detail? Are there any sections that could be condensed?
- Is the writing "voice" appropriate for the information the author is providing?
- What are three suggestions you would give the writer to improve this piece?

If you are having other people read your work for a workshop, there are some questions you should consider before hearing their comments. These questions will help you define your thoughts about your writing and give you a basis for comparing and considering your readers' comments.

- What is the main point, the focus, of this paper?
- How would you describe the writing "voice"?
- What is the strongest part of the paper?
- What is the weakest part of the paper?
- What parts of the paper were the hardest to write?
- What would you work on if you had 24 more hours to spend on the project?
- What three questions would you like to ask your readers?

With the comments from other readers and the ideas you have come up with through cutting and pasting, you should be able to identify any problems you have in the overall structure of your draft or any ideas that need to be developed or explained more completely. You may want to reorganize the paper, shifting ideas or examples for greater clarity or effect. You may need to do some additional research in order to explain your ideas more fully or to provide additional examples or data. You may need to cut sections of the paper that wander from your focus or that unnecessarily repeat information. Or you may need to spend more time explaining and analyzing the information you have in order to answer your readers' questions.

Take the time to do those things now. This is the point at which you need to fine-tune the overall structure of your piece. This is the point at which you have to settle on what information you are providing and how your are providing it. Take the time to do it and to do it right.

Revising For Details

Revising effectively is a continual process of fixing ever smaller problems. After you finished your draft you started the revision process by examining and reworking your structure and ideas. With that accomplished, you can take time to look at the examples and illustrations in your draft. After that, we will look at paragraph structure and transitions. Then we will find and rewrite any weak sentences. Finally, we will try to eliminate unnecessary words and to make sure that you have fixed any grammatical and punctuation problems.

In order to do this, the rest of this chapter contains a number of short exercises that will help you rewrite and refine your paper to make it as precise and engaging as possible.

Examples

The more clearly you can illustrate your ideas through precise and detailed examples and data, the more easily your reader will be able to understand your abstract thoughts.

EXERCISE

Example Check

Read your draft, taking time to note in the margin each idea you present. You may note something in each paragraph, or once a page, or whatever your overall structure dictates.

Check to see if, following each idea, there is a clear, precise, detailed example or illustration of the idea and a clear and thorough explanation of the reasons behind the idea.

If you have several important ideas that are not illustrated through examples or data, go back to your notes or sources and see if you can find something that will fit.

Paragraphs

By now you should have a good sense of how your paper is structured, paragraph by paragraph. Even so, it is worth taking a moment to think again about the purpose that paragraphs serve for your reader and to make sure your paragraphs are accomplishing what they should.

For your reader, a paragraph is a visual indication of when an idea changes. There is no such thing as a "correct" length for a paragraph; some may be a page long, others only a sentence. Still, when you change ideas or opinions, or change from a broad concept to a more specific element of that concept, or change from opinion to an example, or otherwise change the writing in a substantive way, you probably need to start a new paragraph.

EXERCISE

Paragraph Check

If you did the Writer/Reader Analysis, use this to see if each paragraph is centered around its own idea. If you are trying to incorporate too many ideas or examples or opinions in a single paragraph, try separating them.

If you did not do the Writer/Reader Analysis, then read through your draft, summarizing the central idea of each paragraph. Again, create new paragraphs when ideas shift or change.

Transitions

Creating a good transition is like crossing a brook with a friend. It is easier for your friend to hop from one stone to the next if you are holding his hand. In the same way, it is easier for your reader to go from one idea to the next if your transitions help him make the jump.

A transition is not necessarily seamless, but it is comprehensible. If you are moving from one idea to another, or one opinion to another, or one idea to an example, you need a clear transition to make sure your reader makes the jump with you.

You can also think of transition as a bridge. It is always linked to two different ideas—two shores, if you will—but it does not necessarily belong to either of them. From the middle of the bridge you can see both ideas, and it takes you from one to the other.

Look at this example of a good transition in Michael's paper on controlling stress in sports:

> *"Some ways of alleviating anxiety are to increase your mental toughness by using conditioning principles and techniques to produce desired behaviors independent of cognitive mediation.*
>
> *"One of the most commonly used techniques by sports psychologists is called counter-conditioning."*

This transition is effective because Michael introduces a broad concept at the end of the first paragraph and then lets us know he is giving a more specific example in the second paragraph by beginning with the phrase "One of the . . ." He also repeats the word "techniques" as a way of connecting the two ideas.

Here is another of Michael's transitions:

> *"Continually repeating this affirmation, would cause me to gain confidence in my ability to hit my forehand, and my self-image would become positive.*
>
> *"In addition to affirmation, the principles of operant conditioning can be used to change a non-professional athlete's unproductive attitude."*

This time Michael had to lead the reader between paragraphs where the subject changed significantly. Using the phrase "In addition . . ." allowed him to do this clearly and directly.

There are other words that are particularly useful for transitions: *although, yet, for example, consequently, conversely, but, however, also, additionally, still,* and so on.

There are many places where you may need no specific transition; one idea logically leads to the next. But, if it doesn't, make sure not to let go of the reader's hand.

Sentences

Now we are getting to the kind of detailed revision that is time consuming, but vital. Examining your paper sentence by sentence and making sure that each sentence is as clear, precise, and engaging as possible can be long and painstaking—and occasionally frustrating—work. Yet, writing is, at its most essential, simply a series of connected words and sentences. The better your individual sentences, the better your writing.

Each word, each sentence, should be as precise as possible. For example, this sentence:

> *"AIDS is a growing problem among adults in this country."*

is not nearly as clear or precise as:

> *"AIDS is now the leading cause of death among American men between the ages of 25 and 44."*

Or this sentence:

> *"There are problems with the methodology used in the study."*

is not as precise as:

> *"Given the significant number of subjects who did not partici-pate in the post-test procedure—almost 25 percent—it is diffi-cult to draw firm conclusions from the results."*

EXERCISE

Precise Sentences

Find three of your most detailed and precise sentences and write them down on a separate sheet of paper.

Then find three more general, vague sentences and rewrite them with more precision and detail.

Keep looking for vague and general sentences in your paper and, as much as possible, keep turning them into sentences as precise and detailed as the first three you chose.

If you think some sentences in your paper are weaker than others but you are unsure how to fix them, try the following exercise.

EXERCISE

Best and Worst Sentences

Circle the best sentences in your draft—the most precise, the most vivid, the most detailed, the most intelligent, with the strongest sense of voice, or the ones that simply sound good.

Examine the sentences you have circled and, on a separate sheet of paper, write at least five reasons why those sentences are the best; each reason need not apply to every sentence circled.

Now, draw a box around the weakest sentences in your draft.

Examine those sentences and try to write down five reasons why those sentences are less than satisfactory.

Compare the two lists and the two sets of sentences and see what the differences are.

Using the ideas and examples from the best sentences, try to rewrite the weaker sentences to make them sound more like the strongest ones. This may require going back to your notes, combining shorter sentences, or separating longer ones. Be flexible.

Words

In the course of creating more precise sentences, you have no doubt been having to search for more precise words. The two tasks are inseparable. We have talked about how your choice of words affects your writing voice, about how detailed and precise words help your reader to understand exactly what you mean.

There are some problems that individual words can pose, however, that you should be watchful for as you do detailed revision.

First, avoid jargon. This is not an admonition against using specialized language when it is appropriate. If you are trying to be precise, you may need to use words that describe specific concepts in your field. (If you are unsure about whether your audience is familiar with the word, you may need to explain it, however.) For example, the term *cognitive dissonance"* describes a specific psychological concept; it would be next to impossible to write a paper about that concept without using that term.

Yet, academic writing, as with much professional writing, can get bogged down when writers use complicated jargon for its own sake. Instead of using specialized words and terms to enhance the detail and precision of a paper, some writers use complicated words and sentences for more straightforward ideas because they want to try to sound more impressive or to avoid direct statements, or simply because they have not taken the time to make sure their writing is clear and concise.

Don't let yourself slide into the jargon trap. If you are writing about death, don't call it "negative patient outcome." If you are writing about solitary confinement cells in prisons, don't call them "individual behavior adjustment units." If you are writing about civilian casualties in a war, don't call them "collateral damage."

Make sure your writing is clear and direct—and honest.

If useless jargon is one obstacle to clarity in writing, another is wordiness. There is no right or wrong number of words to use in a paper (aside from length restrictions that your professor may place on an assignment). What is more important is that you make every word in your writing count.

Consider the following phrases. What do they have in common?

Due to the fact that

At this point in time

Past history

In the near future

Went on to say

Is of the opinion that

All of the phrases can be reduced to a single word:

Because

Now

History

Soon

Continued

Thinks

If one word can do the job, don't use five. Save those words for the more complex ideas in your paper that cannot be reduced to a single word. Why waste your time with "Due to the fact that" when you can say "Because" and get on to the meat of the sentence?

Don't waste space by inflating simple words into bloated phrases. Getting rid of unnecessary words in minor phrases such as these will allow your reader to focus on the essential and important words in a sentence and paragraph.

EXERCISE

Word Cutting

Read through your draft and cut 10 words. You can simply cut the words, or you can replace wordy phrases with a single word. You should be able to do it without breaking a sweat.

Now cut 10 more. It still shouldn't be too hard.

Then cut 10 more.

You could probably cut 10 more.

Keep your focus on the vital words. Keep everything else to a minimum.

A final thought about words. In order to use them effectively, you have to know what they mean. Occasionally we have students who are concerned that their vocabulary is not extensive enough to write at the college level. They ask us how they can expand their vocabulary to use more effective, more sophisticated words. Our response, that they need to read frequently and widely with a dictionary by their side, seems to be a disappointment. Some of them seem to be looking for a list somewhere to study that will do the trick. Yet, simply seeing a word on a list and knowing its dictionary meaning probably will not add it to the vocabulary you use in your writing assignments. It is reading words in context, and understanding what the words mean, that allows you to use them in your own writing in the proper context. If you want to learn words, read—with a dictionary at your side.

For this same reason we would caution you about using a thesaurus when you write. First, you will not always find exact synonyms in a thesaurus. So, if you don't know the meaning of the new word you may use it incorrectly. Also, as we mentioned before, words with the same denotation may have very different connotations. For example, if you were writing a paper about the psychological concept of "conservation" and looked up that word in a thesaurus you would find the entry to include words such as *maintenance, preservation, storage, salvation,* and *husbanding.*

Also, though the meaning of the word may be, in some instances, similar, it may do very odd things to your writing voice. Trust your own vocabulary. Or, if you feel you need to use a thesaurus, check the words you choose from it with your dictionary.

POLISHING YOUR WRITING

By the time you get to the point of polishing your paper, you may be getting so tired of working on it that you are tempted to just turn it in and hope that if there are any errors no one will notice them. Don't give in to temptation. Taking the extra time to check carefully for possible errors in grammar, spelling, or format is well worth the effort. Every error you leave in a paper erodes your credibility. If you are not careful about the details of your writing, why should your reader trust you to be careful about the details of your research and your conclusions? Any error undermines your work; and you do not want all of the work you put into this paper to be discounted because of errors you could have easily corrected.

If you do not already have one, you should buy a style manual or grammar handbook. Many are available, and most cover much of the same information. Find one that looks as if it will be easy for you to use—then buy it and keep it and your dictionary with you when you write. As with a dictionary, a style manual or grammar handbook is not a publication you will memorize. It is a reference book you should be able to use quickly and effectively.

The other resource you may want to seek when polishing your paper is a good proofreader to read it. Considering the amount of time you have put into this paper, it may, in fact, be getting difficult for you to see the errors (not that you shouldn't try, of course). If you have a friend or classmate who is a good proofreader—in other words, a person who will read carefully and who can recognize errors in spelling and grammar—then by all means seek that person out and have him read the paper.

If you have been writing with a computer, you will probably have access to a spell check program. These can be useful devices; we use them ourselves. They can catch many misspellings and typos. **But beware!** Spell checks are not infallible. They will not be able to determine context. Consequently, if you misspelled "from" as "form" or "here" as "hear" or "their" as "there" or "your" as "you" the computer will not catch the problem. Use a spell check as a final backup, not a replacement for proofreading.

Some Common Problems

Although the best thing for you to do is to buy a style manual or grammar handbook and become familiar with it by using it often, there are several common problems of which you should be particularly aware as you proofread your paper.

Subject-Verb Agreement: Make sure that the verbs in your sentences agree with the subjects. For example:

> *"The increase in violent crimes have caused discipline problems at the school."*

is incorrect. "Increase," not "crimes," is the subject in this sentence. The sentence should read:

> *"The increase in violent crimes has caused discipline problems at the school."*

(Note: Words used in the social sciences such as *data, media, phenomena,* and *criteria* are <u>plural</u> forms of the words *datum, medium, phenomenon,* and *criterion.* Consequently, you use plural verbs with the plural nouns. For example: "The data from this study are inconclusive.")

Pronoun-Antecedent Agreement: The number of the nouns you refer to in a sentence—people or organizations—must agree with the pronoun you choose. For example:

> *"The researcher then recorded their findings in the logbook."*

is incorrect. "Researcher" is singular, so "their" should be replaced by "his" or "her." Or, if appropriate, you could replace "researcher" with "researchers."

The same holds true for organizations. For example:

> *"The committee voted unanimously to give their permission."*

is incorrect. The "committee" is a single unit and, therefore, needs a singular pronoun:

> *"The committee voted unanimously to give its permission."*

(You could replace "committee" with "committee members" and still use the plural pronoun.)

Tense Shifts: Make sure that your use of tense is consistent in your writing. For example:

> *"The researchers conducted the interviews during a two-month period. They find the subjects unwilling to discuss the second half of the survey."*

is incorrect. If the first sentence is in the past tense—"conducted"—then the second sentence should be as well—"found."

Affect/Effect: *Affect* is a verb. *Effect* is a noun. For example:

> *"The effect of the drug was affected by the amount of food the subjects ate."*

Sentence Structure: Each sentence should make sense. Obvious enough. Yet, if you misplace sections of your sentence it may have a meaning you absolutely do not intend. For example:

> *"Having filled out all of the surveys, the researchers thanked their subjects."*

Of course, the researchers didn't fill out the surveys; the subjects did. Read your work carefully. Make sure each sentence actually says what you want it to say.

Punctuation: Perhaps the most important type of error to correct, and often the hardest to catch, involves punctuation. Missing or misplaced punctuation can change the entire meaning of a sentence.

For example:

> *"Local health officials were unaware of the problem for the first year or two. Budget constraints were less of a problem for private hospitals."*

has a very different meaning from:

> *"Local health officials were unaware of the problem. For the first year or two budget constraints were less of a problem for private hospitals."*

Or, for example:

> *"Now that patients have a choice of treatments when before only one had been approved there is the potential for confusion."*

is not nearly as clear as:

> *"Now that patients have a choice of treatments, when before only one had been approved, there is the potential for confusion."*

It may help to think of punctuation as visible breathing. In other words, when we speak, we use pauses and breaths to let other people know where individual thoughts begin and end and how they are connected. When we write, we use punctuation to create sentences to separate these thoughts. It may be helpful to read your paper aloud, making sure that your punctuation coincides with the natural pauses you make when reading.

You know the uses of a period, comma, semicolon, colon, quotation marks, and so on. (If you are unsure about, say, how to use a semicolon, do consult a handbook.) The trick is making sure you use the right one in the right spot.

For example, a fairly common problem we see in papers is what should be two sentences separated by a period being written as one long sentence separated by a comma. (This is called a "comma splice.") For example:

> *"Any person buying a magazine today will not be looking at overweight people, she will, instead, see very thin and attractive models."*

Because these two ideas are distinct and can stand alone, they should be separated by a period instead of a comma. For example:

> *"Any person buying a magazine today will not be looking at overweight people. She will, instead, see very thin and attractive models."*

Or, if you have two distinct ideas that have a close connection, you could separate them with a semicolon. A semicolon is just what it looks like—part period, part comma. For example:

> *"Any person buying a magazine today will not be looking at overweight people; she will, instead, see very thin and attractive models."*

You also need to make sure that you punctuate citations and references correctly. See Appendix B for examples of how to do this.

Once again, you should make use of a grammar handbook and a good proofreader.

MANUSCRIPT FORMAT

Your work as a writer is finished for this paper. It is time to make sure that your work is presented in a clear and readable form. The easier your manuscript is to read, the more your reader will be able to concentrate on your ideas and analysis. Take the time to make sure that your paper conforms to whatever manuscript format your professor requires. If your professor has not given you specific guidelines on how to format your final manuscript, we would suggest you follow the APA guidelines. Here is a brief overview of how to set up your paper and the order in which each section should be presented, according to APA guidelines. (For more detail, again, consult the *Publication Manual of the American Psychological Association.*)

Title Page: You should have a separate title page that includes your title, your name, your institutional affiliation (in this case, your school), a running head, a short title, and a page number. All of these should be double spaced.

The title, name, and school name should be centered in the middle of the page. Try to keep your title short and informative. As with a good lead, a good title will let your reader know the focus of the paper and your position on the issue. A title should be as precise as possible and also should try to attract a reader to read your paper. There is no correct length for titles, though shorter titles are often more effective.

The running head is an abbreviated title of no more than 50 characters. It would be printed at the top of each page if your paper were published in a journal. It should be centered at the bottom of the page. Type: "Running head: FOLLOWED BY THE TITLE IN ALL CAPITAL LETTERS."

The short title, which is the first two or three words of your title (for example: Concept to Completion), goes in the upper-right-hand corner of your title page with the page number underneath it. This will go in the upper-right-hand corner of every page of your paper.

Abstract: As we mentioned in Chapter Three, and as you no doubt found in your research, in the social sciences, many articles and reports have abstracts. These summaries of the articles give other researchers a sense of the purpose and scope of the paper and whether it will serve the purposes of their research. Not all research papers are required to have abstracts, though a formal research report, as outlined in Appendix C, should have an abstract. If you are unsure about whether to write an abstract for your paper, ask your professor.

The abstract should be typed on a separate page following the title page. Type the word "Abstract" centered at the top of the page, skip a line, and type the abstract in one paragraph without indenting.

An abstract needs to be concise—no more than about 120 words. It should contain a one- or two-sentence summary of your focus, an indication of the position or scope of the paper, a sense of the kinds of sources you used in the research, and the conclusions or implications or applications of the paper.

In meeting those criteria, a good abstract should also have several qualities. It should be as clear and precise as possible. If there is one particular source or study you refer to in detail, you should mention it in your abstract. It needs to accurately reflect exactly what is in the paper, and it should be able to stand alone; in other words, you should not have to read the paper to understand the abstract.

Here is an example of an abstract from an academic study about homeless children. Because it is an actual study, rather than a research paper, it contains some information your abstract might not. Even so, it is a good example of a concise, clear summary of the article.

"In this largely exploratory study of the conflict management and coping behavior of homeless adolescents, the authors interviewed 176 families (mother-adolescent dyads) living in New York City welfare hotels. Results indicated that peer conflict was the 'worst' problem of the previous month as reported by approximately 50 percent of these youths. Homeless adolescents demonstrated conflict management and coping patterns that differ in certain respects from adolescent patterns previously described in the literature. The implications of these differences as well as directions for future research are discussed" (Horowitz, Boardman, & Redlener, 1994, p. 85).

Spacing and Margins: Double space the body of your paper and leave one-inch margins on all sides. Use a ribbon that will give you clear, dark print and do not use elaborate typefaces. On the first page of the body of your paper type your title again (centered), skip a line, and begin your paper. Paragraphs should be indented five spaces.

References: Your list of references should be on a separate page at the end of the body of the paper. The page should be titled "References" with the title centered. List the sources alphabetically by the author's last name or the title of the work if no author is listed. Because a paper for a course is usually considered a final copy, you should single space each entry, making the first line flush left and the rest of the lines indented three spaces. For more detail on how to list references, see Appendix B.

Appendixes: In APA style, it is rare to use an appendix at the end of your paper. Yet, you might decide to use an appendix for information that would be beneficial for the reader to have but not vital to the body of the paper. For example, you could use an appendix to describe a piece of equipment used in an experiment; or you could use one to provide a list of interview or survey questions.

Appendixes should be double spaced. Center the title of each followed by a letter in the order in which you mention them in the body of the paper (Appendix A, Appendix B, for example).

Footnotes: You use notes in APA style most often for content that is important to include but that would be distracting to the reader if it came in the middle of the paper. In APA style, content notes come, not at the bottom of the page on which they are referred, but instead on a separate page after the body of the paper. Use a superscript numeral (a numeral just above the line of type) to refer to a note in the body of the paper. Put all the notes on a separate page with the title "Footnotes" centered at the top. Double space the notes, indenting the first line five spaces.

Tables and Figures: Some information may be easier for your reader to understand if you present it in a table or a figure. (If you use a table or a figure from another source you do, of course, have to cite it.) There are two simple rules to keep in mind when using a table or a figure.

First, if you use a table or a figure, don't duplicate all the information it provides in the text of your paper.

Second, on the other hand, don't use a table or a figure without mentioning it in the text and explaining its implications. You don't duplicate the information, but you do interpret it for the reader. Put each table and each figure on a separate page. These will go after the body of your paper and before the references page.

Tables need to be double spaced with the number of the table at the top, left-hand side of the page. Besides the heading at the top of the page (Table 1) you may also want to give each table a title (for example, Mean Numbers of Incorrect Responses by Adults Using Mass Transit).

Figures are photographs, graphs, illustrations, charts, diagrams, maps, and so on. Each figure should go on a separate page with the number of the figure at the top, left-hand side (Figure 1, Figure 2, for example). Captions for figures go on a separate page and are listed in order. For example:

Figure 3: Drawing by subject after 36 hours of sleep deprivation.

THINKING ABOUT THE PROJECT

Congratulations!

Your paper is finished and ready to turn in. Well done. Give yourself a breather and a round of applause. Go, turn your paper in. Come back tomorrow and read the rest of this chapter.

Finishing and turning in this research paper are accomplishments that should make you feel good. Yet, do not let the lessons you learned during the researching and writing of this paper end after you turn it in. This project is over; but there will be other projects in the future. You want to be able to use the writing process you developed in working on this paper to write other papers effectively. To help you do that, take a moment to think in more detail about your writing process.

EXERCISE

Thinking About Your Writing

This is a free-writing exercise. No pressure. It is a chance to focus your thinking on the strengths and weaknesses you discovered in your writing during the past few weeks. Give yourself 10 minutes to write about each of the following questions. Keep your responses where you can find them the next time you are given a writing assignment.

- What went well during this writing project? What part of the writing process did you do most effectively?
- Where did you have problems with your writing during this project? How did you resolve those writing problems?
- What would you do differently if you were to start this project all over again?

Write and Write Well

Nobody ever learns to write. Every good writer is always learning to write. Don't let your learning stop here. We have given you a number of approaches you can use and adapt to help you improve your writing. If, however, you want your writing to continue to improve, you need to continue to develop and refine your writing process.

Always remember three things:

Focus on a main idea; then always keep in mind your focus, your sense of what you want the reader to know.

Write often and early and revise thoroughly, trying to capitalize on your strengths and being aware of your weaknesses.

Read as much good writing as you possibly can.

If you care about your ideas, then you will care about communicating them clearly. That clear communication is the goal of every good writer. Good luck.

Appendix A

Sources in Social
Science Research

Most research will eventually take you to the primary sources that can provide the firsthand theories and data you need to answer the questions posed by your topic. Still, you have to begin somewhere in order to find those primary sources. The following is a partial list of the indexes, directories, databases, encyclopedias, bibliographies, abstracts, and other sources that will help you find the sources that fit your focus.

POTENTIAL RESEARCH SOURCES

ANTHROPOLOGY

Bibliographies and Indexes

International Committee for Social Science Information and Documentation Staff. (1989). *International bibliography of the social sciences: Anthropology.* New York: Routledge.
Social science index. (1974–present). New York: Wilson.
Social sciences citation index.® (1969–present). Philadelphia: Institute for Scientific Information.

Databases

ERIC (Educational Resources Information Center)
SOCIAL SCISEARCH
SOCIOFILE

Encyclopedias and Dictionaries

A dictionary of social science methods. (1983). New York: Wiley.
Hunter, D.E., & Whitten, P. (Eds.). (1976). *Encyclopedia of anthropology.* New York: Harper.

Research Guides and Handbooks

American Psychological Association. (1994). *Publication manual of the American Psychological Association* (4th ed.). Washington, DC: Author.
Judd, C.M., Smith, E.R., & Kidder, L.H. (1991). *Research methods in social relations* (6th ed.). Fort Worth, TX: Holt, Rinehart and Winston.
Park, P., Brydon-Miller, M.L., Hall, B., & Jackson, T. (Eds.). (1993). *Voices of change: Participatory research in the United States and Canada.* Westport, CT: Bergin and Garvey.

PSYCHOLOGY

Bibliographies and Indexes

American Psychological Association. (1968–present). *Cumulative author index to psychological abstracts.* Washington, DC: Author.
American Psychological Association. (1968–present). *Cumulative subject index to psychological abstracts.* Washington, DC: Author.
American Psychological Association. (1969–present). *Index medicus.* Washington, DC: Author.
Bibliographic guide to psychology. (1975–present). Boston: Hall.
Crabtree, J.M., & Moyer, K.E. (1977). *Bibliography of aggressive behavior: A reader's guide to the research literature.* New York: Liss.
Grinstein, A. (Ed.). (1956–71). *The index of psychoanalytic writings.* (14 vols.). New York: International Universities.
The Harvard list of books in psychology (4th Ed.). (1971). Cambridge, MA: Harvard University Press.
Science citation index. (1961–present). Philadelphia: Institute for Scientific Information.
Social science index. (1974–present) New York: Wilson.
Social sciences citation index.® (1969–present). Philadelphia: Institute for Scientific Information.

Abstracts

American Psychological Association. (1927–present). *Psychological abstracts.* Lancaster, PA: Author.
Annual review of psychology. (1950–present). Palo Alto, CA: Annual Review.

Child development abstracts and bibliography. (1927–present). Chicago: University of Chicago Press.
Sage family studies abstracts. (1977–present). San Mateo, CA.

Databases

CHILD ABUSE AND NEGLECT
ERIC (Educational Resources Information Center)
MENTAL HEALTH ABSTRACTS
PAIS (Government and Public Policy)
PSYCHINFO
PsycLIT®
CLINPSYCH
SOCIOFILE

Encyclopedias and Dictionaries

American Psychological Association. (1994). *Thesaurus of psychological index terms* (7th ed.). Washington, DC: Author.
Chaplin, J.P. (1985). *Dictionary of psychology* (rev. ed.). New York: Dell.
Corsini, R.J. (Ed.) (1984). *Encyclopedia of psychology* (4 vols.). New York: Wiley.
A dictionary of social science methods. (1983). New York: Wiley.
Eysneck, H.J. (Ed.). (1984). *Encyclopedia of psychology* (3rd ed.). New York: Continuum.
Gregory, R.L. (Ed.). (1987). *The Oxford companion to the mind.* New York: Oxford University Press.
Harre, R., & Lamb, R. (1983). *Encyclopedic dictionary of psychology.* Cambridge, MA: MIT.
Hinsie, L.E., & Campbell, R.J. (Eds.). (1970). *Psychiatric dictionary.* New York: Oxford University Press.

Research Guides and Handbooks

American Psychological Association. (1994). *Publication manual of the American Psychological Association* (4th ed.). Washington, DC: Author.
Judd, C.M., Smith, E.R., & Kidder, L.H. (1991). *Research methods in social relations* (6th ed.). Fort Worth, TX: Holt, Rinehart and Winston.
McInnis, R.G. (Ed.). (1982). *Research guide for psychology.* Westport, CT: Greenwood.
Marken, R. (1981). *Introduction to psychological research.* Monterey, CA: Brooks.
Park, P., Brydon-Miller, M.L., Hall, B., & Jackson, T. (Eds.). (1993). *Voices of change: Participatory research in the United States and Canada.* Westport, CT: Bergin and Garvey.

Reed, J.G., & Baxter, P.M. (1983). *Library use: A handbook for psychology.* Washington, DC: American Psychological Association.

SOCIAL WORK

Bibliographies and Indexes

Conrad, J.H. (Ed.). (1982). *Reference sources in social work: An annotated bibliography.* Metuchen, NJ: Scarecrow.

Mendelsohn, H.N. (1987). *A guide to information sources for social work and the human services.* Phoenix: Oryx.

Social science index. (1974–present). New York: Wilson.

Social sciences citation index.® (1969–present). Philadelphia: Institute for Scientific Information.

Abstracts

Sage family studies abstracts. (1977–present). San Mateo, CA: Sage.

Social work research and abstracts. (1964–present). New York: National Association of Social Work.

Databases

CHILD ABUSE AND NEGLECT
ERIC (Educational Resources Information Center)
FAMILY RESOURCES
PSYCHINFO
PsycLIT®
SOCIAL SCISEARCH
SOCIOFILE

Encyclopedias and Dictionaries

A dictionary of social science methods. (1983). New York: Wiley.

Fairchild, H.P. (Ed.) (1977). *Dictionary of sociology and related sciences.* Totowa, NJ: Littlefield.

Minahan, A. (Ed.) *Encyclopedia of social work* (3 vols.). Silver Spring, MD: National Association of Social Work.

Research Guides and Handbooks

American Psychological Association. (1994). *Publication manual of the American Psychological Association* (4th ed.). Washington, DC: Author.

Bart, P.B., & Frankel, L. (1981). *Student sociologist's handbook* (3rd Ed.). Glenview, IL: Scott.

Judd, C.M., Smith, E.R., & Kidder, L.H. (1991). *Research methods in social relations* (6th ed.). Fort Worth, TX: Holt, Rinehart and Winston.

Park, P., Brydon-Miller, M.L., Hall, B., & Jackson, T. (Eds.). (1993). *Voices of change: Participatory research in the United States and Canada.* Westport, CT: Bergin and Garvey.

SOCIOLOGY

Bibliographies and Indexes

Combined retrospective index to journals in sociology, 1895–1974. (1978). Woodbridge, CT: Research Publications.

Mark, C., & Mark, P.F. (1976). *Sociology of America: A guide to informative sources.* Detroit: Gale.

Social science index. (1974–present). New York: Wilson.

Social sciences citation index.® (1969–present). Philadelphia: Institute for Scientific Information.

Sociology: Classification schedule, author and title listing, chronological listings, (2 vols.). (1973). Cambridge, MA: Harvard University Press.

Abstracts

Sociological abstracts. (1953–present). New York: Sociological Abstracts.

Databases

CHILD ABUSE AND NEGLECT
ERIC (Educational Resources Information Center)
NCJRS (National Criminal Justice Reference Service)
PAIS (Government and Public Policy)
PSYCHINFO
PsycLIT®
SOCIAL SCISEARCH
SOCIOFILE

Encyclopedias and Dictionaries

A dictionary of social science methods. (1983). New York: Wiley.

Encyclopedic dictionary of sociology (4th ed.). (1991). Guilford, CT: Dushkin.

Fairchild, H.P. (Ed.). (1977). *Dictionary of sociology and related sciences.* Totowa, NJ: Littlefield.

Jary, D., & Jary, J. (1991). *The HarperCollins dictionary of sociology.* New York: Harper.

The thesaurus of sociological research terms (3rd ed.). (1992). San Diego: Sociological Abstracts, Inc.

Research Guides and Handbooks

American Psychological Association. (1994). *Publication manual of the American Psychological Association* (4th ed.). Washington, DC: Author.

Bart, P.B., & Frankel, L. (Eds.). (1981). *Student sociologist's handbook* (3rd ed.). Glenview, IL: Scott.

Judd, C.M., Smith, E.R., & Kidder, L.H. (1991). *Research methods in social relations* (6th ed.). Fort Worth, TX: Holt, Rinehart and Winston.

Park, P., Brydon-Miller, M.L., Hall, B., & Jackson, T. (Eds.). (1993). *Voices of change: Participatory research in the United States and Canada.* Westport, CT: Bergin and Garvey.

Appendix B

Reference and Citation Formats for APA and MLA

Accurate and complete citations and references will help your readers understand your work, just as you used the citations and references of others to do your research. Although the principles of internal citation forms are simple, as we discussed in Chapter Four, it is helpful to see specific examples of how those forms work. Again, if you require more detailed or specialized information on citation and reference format, use the *Publication Manual of the American Psychological Association, fourth edition.*

APA STYLE

How to punctuate internal citations

Parenthetical citations are included within the sentences to which they refer.

Commas separate the name from the date in a citation.

Use the word "and" when you mention two authors in the text; but use an ampersand (&) when more than one name appears in a citation.

Use "p." and "pp." as abbreviations for "page" and "pages" in a citation.

Citation Format

If you mention the author's name in the text:
Put the year of publication in parentheses immediately after the name.

Craybill (1978) found that children with high self-esteem describe their parents as encouraging psychological autonomy and as psychologically accepting.

If the source has two authors, note both names:
According to Harper and Hoelter (1987), empirical research has shown that perceived appraisal by parents (measured directly) does, in fact, affect self-esteem.

If the author's name is not mentioned in the text:
Then you need to put the author's name in the citation.
Rapists, on the other hand, tend to demonstrate an ability to have otherwise healthy adult relationships (Gelman, 1990).

If the source has two authors:
Although the programs vary in their approach and duration, each targets particular risk factors such as low self-esteem, poor communication and social skills, unhealthy attitudes towards sexuality and women, and deviant sexual arousal patterns (Gordon & Porporino, 1991).

If the source has more than two authors, but fewer than six authors:
Cite all the authors the first time the reference occurs. After that, cite only the last name of the first author followed by "et al." and the year of publication.
Similarly, negative parental behaviors such as inconsistent control and coercion lead the child to question his or her own worth (Barber, Chadwick, & Oerter, 1992).
For middle-class, white, American families, perceived parental behavior can reliably predict child self-esteem (Barber et al., 1992).

If the source has more than six authors:
Use the last name of the first author and "et al." on every reference.

If you quote directly from a source:
Add the page number to your citation.
Gecas and Schwalbe (1986) write, "Parental behavior that indicates positive evaluation of the child, such as support participation, and interest in the child, should be positively correlated to self-esteem (p. 38)."
Or
"Counselors at the clinic have caseloads of about thirty patients. They say it is too many, that they don't have enough time to spend with patients (Kirn, 1990, p. 2975)."

If the author is a government agency or other organization:
Put the full name in the first reference, followed by the abbreviation in brackets. Use the abbreviation in the references that follow.
A new study (National Institute of Mental Health [NIMH], 1991) was conducted the following year.
The results of the survey (NIMH, 1991) were the same.

If the work has no author listed:
Cite the first two or three words of the title of the work. If it is an article or chapter title put it in quotation marks. If it is a book title, underline it.

Fourteen centers closed in 1990 alone ("Budget cuts," 1991).

If you need to list more than one source in a citation:
Put them in the same parentheses in alphabetical order by the first author's last name. Separate the sources by semicolons.

This contradicts the previous research (Demo, Small, & Savin-Williams, 1987; Gecas & Schwalbe, 1986).

If two authors have the same last name:
Include their initials in all references to avoid confusion.

B.A. Johnson (1992) and L.W. Johnson (1989) also found similar results.

If your source was mentioned in another author's work:
You indicate the source where you found the information.

Coopersmith also argued that self-esteem is influenced by, "first and foremost the amount of respectful, accepting, and concerned treatment that an individual receives from the significant others in this life" (cited in Braithwaite, 1983, p. 154).

Note: You would put Braithwaite's, not Coopersmith's, work in your list of references because that is where you found the information.

If you need to cite an interview or personal communication (letters, memos, phone calls, etc.):
You would not put these sources in your list of references because they are not recoverable data. You cite them in the text only and give the initials of the source and the date of the communication.

Some patients require medical or psychological attention, some require special counselling for physical or sexual abuse, and some require primarily drug or alcohol counselling (J. Myers, personal interview, October 5, 1992).

Reference Format

A reference list contains only those works that are cited in a paper. (A bibliography may contain works for background or further reading.) All works that are cited must be in the reference list.

List sources alphabetically by the first author's last name. If the author's name is not known, list the work alphabetically by the first word of the title (ignoring "A," "An," or "The").

Use only initials, not first names, for authors (unless two people have the same last names and initials).

For works with multiple authors, list all names, last name first, followed by initials.

For edited works, add the abbreviation "Ed." after the editor's last name and initials. For multiple editors, the abbreviation "Eds." comes after the last editor's name.

The year of publication, in parentheses, follows the author's name. If you use two or more sources by the same author, list them chronologically. If the two sources appeared in the same year, list them alphabetically by title and use letters (a, b, c, d) next to the publication date to distinguish between the works.

Punctuation

Underline or italicize book titles, periodical titles, and volume numbers.

Article titles and chapter names are not underlined, italicized or put in quotation marks.

Capitalize only the first word and proper nouns in book or article titles. Capitalize all the primary words in a periodical title.

Put commas between an author's last name and initials and between authors' names. Put an ampersand (&) before the final author's name.

Put periods between the main parts of an entry. For a book: author. (date). title. city of publication: publisher. For a journal article: author. (date). title of article. name of publication, volume number, page numbers.

Start the first line of each reference flush left and indent the following lines three spaces.

Examples

A journal article with one author
Terrace, H.S. (1985). In the beginning was the "name." American Psychologist, , 1011-1028.

A journal article with two authors
Hansen, C. & Hansen, R. (1988). Finding the face in the crowd: An anger superiority effect. *Journal of Personality and Social Psychology, 54,* 917-924.

A journal article with more than two authors
Stigler, J.W., Barclay, C., & Aiello, P. (1982). Motor and mental abacus skill: A preliminary look at an expert. *Quarterly Newsletter of the Laboratory of Comparative Human Cognition, 4 (1),* 12-14.

Note: The preceding example is from a journal that is not paginated continuously. In other words, most periodicals start with page 1 in the first issue of the year and have consecutive page numbers for the rest of the year's issues. A few periodicals, however, start a new page 1 with each issue. For those, as in the preceding example, put the issue number in parentheses after the volume number.

A magazine or newspaper article
Gelman, D. (1990, July 23). The mind of the rapist. *Newsweek,* pp. 46-52.

An article with no author listed
Citizen's group warns public of convict's release from prison. (1994, August 21). *The New York Times,* p. 44.

A book
Miller, A.G. (1986). *The obedience studies: A case study of controversy in social science.* New York: Praeger.

A book with an editor
Bond, M.H. (Ed.). (1988). *The cross-cultural challenge to social psychology.* Newbury Park, CA: Sage.

A book in translation
Freire, P. (1970). *Pedagogy of the oppressed.* (M.B. Ramos, Trans.). New York: Seabury Press.

A book in an edition other than the first
Judd, C.M., Smith, E.R., & Kidder, L.H. (1991). *Research methods in social relations* (6th ed.). Fort Worth, TX: Holt, Rinehart and Winston.

A chapter in a book with an editor
Campos, J., Hiatt, S., Ramsay, D., Henderson, C., & Svejda, M. (1978). The emergence of fear on the visual cliff. In M. Lewis & L.A. Rosenblum (Eds.), *The development of affect.* New York: Plenum Press.

A book with a corporate author
The World Bank. (1984). *World development report 1984.* New York: Oxford University Press.

A publication with no author listed
Final report of the Commission on the Higher Education of Minorities. (1982). Los Angeles: Higher Education Research Institute.

A book review
Gold, J.R. (1994). [Review of *Defenses in psychotherapy: The clinical application of the defense mechanisms inventory].* *Journal of Personality Assessment, 63,* 191-193.

A published interview

Hall, E. (1983, September). A cure for American education. [Interview with B.F. Skinner]. *Psychology Today, 17,* p. 26.

A government document

U.S. Department of Justice. (1985). *Crime in the United States 1984.* Washington, DC: U.S. Government Printing Office.

A dissertation abstract

Poremba, G.A. (1990). The impacts of federal, state, and local fiscal austerity on Washington county service agencies. *Dissertation Abstracts International, 51,* 3244A.

A dissertation

Hall, A.V. (1991). And then there were three: A parental preparation program for couples expecting their first child. (Doctoral dissertation, Rutgers University). *Dissertation Abstracts International, 52,* 6659B.

Proceedings of a conference

Callaway, H. (Ed.) (1981). Case studies of participatory research. *Proceedings of the International Forum on Participatory Research. Ljubljana, Yugoslavia, 1980.* Amersfoot, the Netherlands: Netherlands Center for Research and Development in Adult Education.

An unpublished paper presented at a meeting

Horton, B. (1981). *On the potential of participatory research: An evaluation of a regional experiment.* Paper presented at Annual Meeting of the Society for the Study of Social Problems, Toronto.

A film or videotape

Child Care Employee Project. (1991). *Worthy work, worthless wages* [Videotape]. Oakland, CA: Author.

A television broadcast

Public Broadcasting System. (1985, June 25). Adam Smith in the new China: From Marx to Mastercard [Television broadcast].

A computer program

Witherspoon, J. (1987). The brain [Computer program]. New York: Harper and Row.

MLA STYLE

Using Modern Language Association (MLA) style is essentially the same as using APA style. It is an internal citation format. If you need to understand it in more detail, consult the *MLA Handbook for Writers of Research Papers.*

MLA style has two significant differences. First, you use citations only when you use a direct quotation, paraphrase, or summary in your text. Also, you don't put the year of publication in the parentheses. Instead, you put the page number where the direct quotation or paraphrase can be found.

For example:

According to Norman, "Parental attitudes and encouragement have perhaps the strongest influence on a student's performance, followed closely by the encouragement of teachers" (408).

Or

Although such development is only beginning, a number of alternative tests and methodologies are currently available that are at least as reliable and inexpensive as the animal techniques they replace (Diner, 3).

Other differences are:

If you use more than one source by the same author, when you cite the author's sources, include enough of the titles of the works to distinguish between them.

For example: (Domhoff, Who Really, 34-45) and (Domhoff, Who Rules, 23).

If you cite a work by more than one author, list the authors by their last names. Use "and" before the last author's name. If there are more than four authors, list the first author's last name and "et al."

If you use a source quoted in another book, cite it in the source where you found it. For example: (qtd. in Smith).

Works Cited Format

In MLA style, the list of references is called a "List of Works Cited." The primary differences from APA style concern the placement of the year of publication, the use of first names, and capitalization of words in titles.

A journal article with one author

Gardner, Frances M. "The Quality of Joint Activity Between Mothers and Their Children with Behavior Problems." *The Journal of Child Psychology and Psychiatry* 35 (1994): 935-948.

A journal article with two authors

Platt, Gerald M., and Rhys H. Williams. "Religion, Ideology, and Electoral Politics." *Society* 25 (1988): 38-45.

A journal article with more than two authors

Miralao, Virginia A., and Luisa T. Engracia. "In the Throes of Transition: Fertility Trends and Patterns in the Phillipines." *Phillipine Sociological Review* 37.3-4 (1989): 26-49.

Note: The preceding example is from a journal that is not paginated continuously. In other words, most periodicals start with page 1 in the first issue of the year and have consecutive page numbers for the rest of the year's issues. A few periodicals, however, start a new page 1 with each issue. For those, as in the preceding example, put the issue number in parentheses after the volume number.

A journal article with more than six authors
Martin, Patricia Yancey, et al. "Work-family Policies: Corporate, Union, Feminist, and Pro-family Leaders' Views." *Gender & Society* 2 (1988): 385–400.

A magazine or newspaper article
Hampton, Pat. "Annie, State's Oldest Inmate, Dead at 100." *The Columbus Dispatch* 23 Jan. 1986: 1A.

An article with no author listed
"How Dull Can You Be?" *Time* 14 Jan. 1991: 45.

A book
Hartford, William. *Working People of Holyoke.* New Brunswick, NJ: Rutgers University Press, 1989.

Two or more books by the same author
Domhoff, G. William. *Who Really Rules?* Santa Monica, CA: Goodyear Publishing Company, 1978.
—. *Who Rules America Now?* New York: Simon and Schuster, 1983.

A book with an editor
Rosenthal, Evelyn R., ed. *Women, Aging and Ageism.* Binghamton, New York: the Haworth Press, 1990.

A book in translation
Freire, Paulo. *The Pedagogy of the Oppressed.* Trans. Myra Bergman Ramos. New York: Seabury Press, 1970.

A book in an edition other than the first
Judd, Charles M., Elliot R. Smith, and Louise H. Kidder. *Research Methods in Social Relations.* 6th ed. Fort Worth, TX: Holt, Rinehart and Winston, 1991.

A chapter in a book with an editor
Kenniston, Kenneth. "Working Mothers." *Marriage and Family in a Changing Society.* Ed. James M. Henslin. 2nd ed. New York: Free Press, 1985. 319–321.

A book by a corporate author
Nebraska Sociological Feminist Collective. *A Feminist Ethic for Social Science Research.* Lewiston, NY and Queenstown, Ontario: the Edward Mellen Press, 1988.

A publication with no author listed
Final report of the Commission on the Higher Education of Minorities. Los Angeles: Higher Education Research Institute, 1982.

A book review
Phelps, LeAdelle. "Lions, Tigers, and Bears." Rev. of *Strategic Family Play Therapy,* by Schlomo Ariel. *Journal of School Psychology* 32 (1994): 313–315.

A personal interview
Myers, Jim. Personal interview. 5 Oct. 1992.

A published interview
Skinner, B.F. Interview. "A Cure for American Education." By Elizabeth Hall. *Psychology Today* Sept. 1983: 26.

A government document
United States Dept. of Health and Human Services. *Surgeon General's Report on Nutrition and Health.* Washington: GPO, 1988.

A dissertation abstract
Hall, Angela Vitello. "And Then There Were Three: A Parental Preparation Program for Couples Expecting Their First Child." *DAI* 52 (1992): 6659B. Rutgers U.

A dissertation
Williams, Gwyneth Irene. "The Politics of Joint Custody." Diss. Princeton U., 1989.

Proceedings of a conference
Callaway, Helen, ed. *Case Studies of Participatory Research. Proceedings of the International Forum on Participatory Research. Ljubljana, Yugoslavia, 1980.* Amersfoot, The Netherlands: Netherlands Center for Research and Development in Adult Education, 1981.

An unpublished paper presented at a meeting
Horton, Billy D. "On the Potential of Participatory Research: An Evaluation of a Regional Experiment."Paper presented at Annual Meeting of the Society for the Study of Social Problems, Toronto, 1981.

A film or videotape
Worthy Work, Worthless Wages. Videotape. Child Care Employee Project,
   1991. 15 min.

A television broadcast
Adam Smith in the New China: From Marx to Mastercard. PBS. 25 June
   1985.

A computer program
Witherspoon, James. *The Brain.* Computer software. New York: Harper and
   Row, 1987.

Appendix C

Writing Projects Beyond the Research Paper

The focus of this book has been on writing a research paper or report. There are, however, a number of other types of writing you may be required to do while you are in school and after you graduate. This Appendix discusses a number of these types of writing and the special requirements of each. We will also make suggestions for other sections of the book you might want to review before beginning one of these projects.

Many programs in psychology and sociology require students to take a course in experimental or research methods. If you are in such a course, you may be required to conduct and report on an experiment or study of some kind.

RESEARCH PROPOSALS

Before an experiment or study is conducted you must develop a proposal outlining the scope of research to be undertaken. In a formal research setting, this proposal would be submitted to a funding source in order to obtain the resources necessary to carry out the work. Yet, less formal, student-generated projects also often require the submission of a proposal.

In addition to allowing a funding agency to determine the merit of the research and to award funds, the proposal also insures that the research to be carried out meets ethical guidelines established to protect animal and human subjects.

A proposal should provide a rationale for the research to be conducted and descriptions of the methods to be used. Often you will be asked to address specific ethical guidelines and to discuss the broader implications of the research. Preparing a careful and complete research proposal not only

135

improves the chances that the research will be funded, but also, like a good focus statement, clarifies what you will do and why. In many cases in which funding is being sought, you will receive a request for proposals (RFP), which outlines in some detail exactly what information is required and in what order it should be presented. Whether applying for research funds or other types of grants, you should be careful to follow these guidelines as closely as possible because to fail to do so can result in the disqualification of the proposal or, at the very least, may make it difficult for the person reading the proposal to locate and evaluate pertinent information.

In general, the proposal follows the same format as the first three elements of the research report, which we describe in the next section. Briefly, however, it begins with an introduction stating the focus of the research. This is followed by a review of pertinent literature in the field. The statement of the specific research hypothesis (or hypotheses) that you will be testing follows and should grow out of the material presented in the literature review. Finally, you should present the experimental procedures, including a discussion of subject selection and a precise description of all experimental methods.

EXPERIMENTS AND STUDY REPORTS

After you have conducted the research, you may use the material described earlier as the basis for your research report. In reporting the results of an experimental research project of this type, a standard format is generally used. This format helps to organize the material so that other readers know exactly where to look for specific kinds of information. The basic outline would be as follows:

Abstract

Introduction

    Review of the Literature

    Statement of Hypotheses

Methods

    Subjects

    Procedures

Results

Discussion

Conclusions

It may help you to think of the overall organization of the experimental report as an hourglass—wide at the top, narrowing at the middle, then wide again at the bottom. The introduction and literature review should first present the most general information—the historical and theoretical foundations for the work you are carrying out. As you continue, your focus should narrow to a discussion of the specific research that led to your study and the development of the instruments you will be using.

The methods and results sections are the narrowest part of the hourglass, dealing with nothing beyond the scope of the research or experiment being presented. The discussion and conclusion sections then reverse the process to move from a presentation of specific analyses to a consideration of the broader implications of the research. General to specific, specific to general. More detailed descriptions of each component of the experimental report follow.

Abstract: You are already familiar with writing an abstract from Chapter Five. In writing an abstract about an experiment or study you will want to include these two additional pieces of information:

1. A brief statement of how the study was conducted. Who were the subjects in the study? What tasks did they perform?
2. What were the major findings of the study?

You should still limit the length of the abstract to a short summary of the project—a maximum of about 120 words—but it should be enough to allow the reader to judge if he wants to read the rest of your paper. For more information on writing an abstract, see Chapter Five.

Introduction: The opening sentence of the introduction, or of the lead, as we called it earlier, should serve both to capture the reader's interest and to inform the reader of the main focus of the research. Review the information on leads in Chapter Five for suggestions on how to approach this section of the paper.

Remember that there is no law that says that writing up an experiment must be boring. Consider the introduction to Milgram's classic study on obedience. He describes why the work is relevant by drawing parallels to the Holocaust.

> "These inhumane policies may have originated in the mind of a single person, but they could only be carried out on a massive scale if a very large number of persons obeyed orders" (Milgram, 1963/1994, p. 371).

How can you fail to find this important and intriguing?

Literature Review: After an initial section describing the focus of the study, you will want to provide a fairly detailed review of the theory and research that have preceded your study. No study or experiment comes out of a vacuum. The research process is developmental, which means that our ideas of what to study and how to go about studying it evolve from our knowledge of earlier research. In describing an experiment it is important to document this earlier work and to show the reader why it is relevant and how it leads to the study or experiment you have done. The process for researching and reporting information for a literature review is essentially the same as that described for the research paper in the earlier chapters. The only real difference is that the focus of the literature review is most often very limited and presents only the information directly related to the study or experiment you are discussing. As described earlier, the literature review should begin with a presentation of the broader theoretical issues being studied, then move to a more focused presentation of the specific studies and methods that have helped to shape your research. As you review your literature review, ask yourself:

1. Does it explain why the research is important?
2. Does it justify the statement of hypotheses?
3. Does it explain why I have chosen a particular approach for conducting this study?

Statement of Hypotheses: At the end of the introduction, following the literature review, you will want to include your statement of hypotheses. An experimental hypothesis is a specific statement of expectation. Based on what you know about the research from your literature review, what do you predict will happen in your experiment or study?

As an example, in Etaugh and Birdoes' study, "Effects of Age, Sex, and Marital Status on Person Perception," included in Lesko's *Readings in Social Psychology* (1994), the authors state their experimental hypothesis in this way: "This study tested the hypothesis that those who occupy the most common marital status for their age and sex will be viewed most positively" (p. 52). This is really the rationale for the work, the question you wish to address, and you will return to it in discussing your results and in your discussion and conclusion sections.

Methods: The methods section describes how you went about conducting the study or experiment. You generally begin by describing who took part in the study and who the experimental subjects were. The subjects might be animal or human depending on the research. With human subjects, you should describe how the subjects were contacted and what criteria were used to select those subjects. It is important to note age, sex, race, nationality, and other information about the subjects that might influence how they responded to the study.

The procedures section that follows the description of subjects should outline in specific detail how the study was conducted. You should describe what specific characteristics or behaviors you were measuring in your study, the independent and dependent variables, and how they were measured. If you used a particular test or survey instrument, for example, this should be described, and information about the reliability and validity of the measure should be provided. (If you are unfamiliar with these terms, they refer to how "good" the measure is, and you can learn more about how this is determined by consulting a research methods text. See Appendix A for some titles.) You should also describe what happened during the course of the experiment or study: what instructions were given to subjects, in what environment did the study take place, and so on. Finally, you should provide a description of how the ethical guidelines for research were met. Information about these guidelines can also be found in any research methods text.

Having completed this section you might ask yourself, "Based on my description, could another researcher conduct the study in precisely the same manner?" This is the ultimate test of a good methods section.

Results: After you have described how the study was conducted, you will want to describe the results you obtained. This section will include both descriptive information and the results of any statistical tests you have performed. For each hypothesis you have stated, you will want to present specific information that addresses that question. You may want to include tables or figures that present the information in graphic form, as well. In general, you do not analyze or discuss the implications of the results in this section, but rather you provide a clear and concise reporting of the data you have collected. You might find it useful to review the sections of Chapter Five about using examples, tables, and figures in your work.

Discussion and Conclusions: Now you can begin to discuss the implications of the results you described in the previous section. What does it all mean? Is it consistent with your hypotheses or statements of expectations? Here you can suggest ways in which your results might be generalized to a wider population, and you can speculate as to the results of future research. But all of this should be tied to the actual results of your study. Finally, what contribution has this study made to the field; why was your work important? What do the results suggest in terms of future research? What are the implications of your work in addressing important issues in the field or in solving social problems? The section in Chapter Five on endings could be useful in helping you write this section of the report.

ANNOTATED BIBLIOGRAPHIES

An annotated bibliography draws together references about a particular subject and provides a brief description of each work cited. If you were to take the reference section from your research paper and draft a brief summary of each work included, this would be an annotated bibliography. In fact, you may find it useful, particularly when dealing with a large number of sources, to create your own annotated bibliography as a step in writing a major research paper or thesis. This is especially true if you are doing research in an area you may return to later. For example, you are doing a paper for a class on some aspect of the criminal justice system, and you have decided to continue your studies in this area. Consider how useful it might be when you are writing another paper in this field to have access to a list of references with information about each one readily available. In fact, as we noted in our discussion of the research process in Chapter Three, many such bibliographies are published and available as references. Information about formatting bibliographies can be found in Appendix B. You can use the information on writing an abstract in this appendix and in Chapter Five as guidelines for summaries of the works cited.

IN-CLASS AND TAKE-HOME ESSAYS

Possibly the most common form of academic writing from the student's perspective is the in-class essay. You have probably been writing these for years, but we thought a few tips from the perspective of the professor might be useful.

First, read and respond to the entire question. If a question is worth 10 points on a test, many professors assign a portion of that total to each part of the question. Leave a part out, lose the points. If you have any questions about what is expected, ask. What may seem straightforward to us may not be as clear to you. The worst that can happen is that the professor will say that she can't answer the question; no harm in asking. Before you go into the test, you might want to review the section in Chapter Two on reading and understanding the assignment.

Second, before you start writing, take a few minutes to jot down a quick outline of your response to the question. What will be your main points? In what order do you want to make these points? What examples will you use to support them? It is always a good idea to present the most important information first; you don't want to run out of time without having covered the main points and most important examples.

This leads us to our third suggestion: Be specific and give examples from the readings and lectures. Of course, we want to know what you think, but you should be prepared to support your opinion with references to the theory and research you have been learning.

Finally, reread both the question and your answer after you finish writing. You may find that you have left out a portion of the question, or something you have written may not be altogether clear, and this will give you a chance to complete and clarify your work.

And, please, try to write legibly. It may sound trivial, but it makes a difference to our sanity and failing eyesight. Besides, what we can't read, we can't grade.

The same guidelines apply to doing a take-home essay. Be sure that you understand what the professor is asking, define a clear focus, address all parts of the question, and support your ideas with detailed examples. Use the sections in Chapter Five on revising and polishing your writing to help you with such assignments.

JOURNALS AND REACTION PAPERS

Increasingly students are being asked to reflect on the material they are learning in more personal ways, either through journals or reaction papers. In a course on environmental psychology, for example, you might be asked to keep a journal recording your reactions to the various physical environments you encounter as a way of making you more aware of the psychological and social impact that the physical environment can have. It is true that the professor has no way of knowing whether you kept the journal on a daily basis, as assigned, or sat down with a bunch of different pens and varied your handwriting in doing the assignment the night before it was due. Still, you will get less out of the assignment doing it this way, and your work will lack the immediacy and detail it would have had if you had reflected on the experience soon after it had happened. Beware: Some of us get around this tendency toward procrastination by collecting journals on a random basis.

Reaction papers are means of encouraging students to integrate the material they are learning in class with their own experience and opinions. The same advice we gave about essay questions applies here. Be sure your work reflects the material to which you are supposed to respond. If a professor asks you to discuss the impact of viewing violence on aggressive behavior and what you think should be done to address this problem, don't go off on a tirade about how much you hate watching hockey. Here, as in any other kind of writing, a clear focus is essential. Answer the question. Demonstrate that you know the material and can apply this knowledge in reaching an informed opinion concerning the question.

WRITE WELL, WHATEVER THE TASK

Certainly there are many other kinds of writing you may be called upon to do in school and on the job—case study reports, client interview summaries, work reports. Keep in mind that the essentials of effective writing are always the same; you want to communicate to a specific audience clearly and convincingly. If you approach each writing assignment with this in mind, you will never fail to get your ideas heard and understood.

References

American Psychological Association. (1994). *Publication manual of the American Psychological Association* (4th ed.). New York: Author.

Andreasen, N.C., Arndt, S., Swayze, V., Cizadlo, T., Flaum, M., O'Leary, D., Ehrhardt, J.C., & Yuh, W.T.C. (1994, October 14). Thalamic abnormalities in schizophrenia visualized through magnetic resonance image averaging. *Science, 266,* 294–298.

Bailey, W.C., & Peterson, R.D. (1994, Summer). Murder, capital punishment, and deterrence: A review of the evidence and an examination of police killings. *Journal of Social Issues, 50,* (2), 53–74.

Ballenger, B.P. (1994). *The curious researcher: A guide to writing research papers.* Needham Heights, MA: Allyn and Bacon.

Brydon-Miller, M.L. (1993). Breaking down barriers: Accessibility self-advocacy in the disabled community. In P. Park, M.L. Brydon-Miller, B. Hall, & T. Jackson, (Eds.), *Voices of change: Participatory research in the United States and Canada.* Westport, CT: Bergin and Garvey.

Cannady, K. (1994, Winter). Alcohol abuse: A Greek obsession? *Signet of Phi Sigma Kappa* (pp. 4–5).

Cohen, D., & Eisdorfen, C. (1983). *Loss of self.* New York: W.W. Norton.

Dale, C. (1993). *Manchester Hispanic Americans: Profile of a hidden community.* Alliance for the Progress of Hispanic Americans. Manchester, NH.

Elbow, P., & Belanoff, P. (1989). *A community of writers: A workshop course in writing.* New York: Random House.

Etaugh, C., & Birdoes, L.N. (1994). Effects of age, sex, and marital status on person perception. In W.A. Lesko (Ed.), *Readings in social psychology* (2nd ed.). Needham Heights, MA: Allyn and Bacon. (Original work published 1991.)

Gibaldi, J., & Achtert, W.S. (Eds). (1988). *MLA handbook for writers of research papers* (3rd ed.). New York: Modern Language Association.

Gibbs, N. (1990, March 19). Love and let die. *Time,* pp. 62–71.

Goffman, E. (1963). *Stigma.* Englewood Cliffs, NJ: Prentice-Hall.

Hock, R. R. (1992). *Forty studies that changed psychology.* Englewood Cliffs, NJ: Prentice-Hall.

Horowitz, S.V., Boardman, S.K., & Redlener, I. (1994). Constructive conflict management and coping in homeless children and adolescents. *Journal of Social Issues, 50* (1), 85–98.

Hyde, J.S. (1984). Children's understanding of sexist language. *Developmental Psychology, 26* (4), 697—706.

Jacobs, R.H. (1990). Friendships among old women. In E.R. Rosenthal (Ed.), *Women, aging and ageism.* New York: the Haworth Press.

Katz, W., & Sternberg-Katz, L. (1992). *Magazines for libraries* (7th ed.). New Providence, NJ: R.R. Bowker.

Lawton, L., Silverstein, M., & Bengston, V. (1994, February). Affection, social contact, and geographic distance between adult children and their parents. *Journal of Marriage and the Family, 56,* 57–68.

Magner, D.K. (1991, March 13). As spring break nears, Surgeon General opens campaign to curb alcohol abuse. *The Chronicle of Higher Education, 37,* p. A32.

Manktelow, K.I., & Over, D.E. (1990). *Inference and understanding: A philosophical and psychological perspective.* London: Routledge.

Milgram, S. (1994). Behavioral study of obedience. In W.A. Lesko (Ed.), *Readings in social psychology* (2nd ed.). Needham Heights, MA: Allyn and Bacon. (Original work published 1963.)

Moulton, J., Robinson, G.U., & Elias, C. (1978). Psychology in action: Sex bias in language use: "Neutral" pronouns that aren't. *American Psychologist, 33,* 1032–1036.

Murray, D.M. (1991). *The craft of revision.* Fort Worth, TX: Holt, Rinehart and Winston.

Rosenthal, J. (1993, August 1). Tongue tide. *The New York Times Magazine,* p. 12.

Segall, M. H., Dasen, P.R., Berry, J.W., & Poortinga, Y.H (1990). *Human behavior in global perspective: An introduction to cross-cultural psychology.* Elmsford, NY: Pergamon Press.

Index